DR BARBARA

NATURAL COOKBOOK

Improve Health and Reduce Inflammation with Extraordinary Recipes Inspired by Dr. Barbara. 100% Natural | Premium Edition

Kristine Ariyah

© **Copyright 2024 by Kristine Ariyah - All rights reserved.**

The following book is provided below with the aim of delivering information that is as precise and dependable as possible. However, purchasing this book implies an acknowledgment that both the publisher and the author are not experts in the discussed topics, and any recommendations or suggestions contained herein are solely for entertainment purposes. It is advised that professionals be consulted as needed before acting on any endorsed actions.

This statement is considered fair and valid by both the American Bar Association and the Committee of Publishers Association, and it holds legal binding throughout the United States.

Moreover, any transmission, duplication, or reproduction of this work, including specific information, will be deemed an illegal act, regardless of whether it is done electronically or in print. This includes creating secondary or tertiary copies of the work or recorded copies, which are only allowed with the express written consent from the Publisher. All additional rights are reserved.

The information in the following pages is generally considered to be a truthful and accurate account of facts. As such, any negligence, use, or misuse of the information by the reader will result in actions falling solely under their responsibility. There are no scenarios in which the publisher or the original author can be held liable for any difficulties or damages that may occur after undertaking the information described herein.

Additionally, the information in the following pages is intended solely for informational purposes and should be considered as such. As fitting its nature, it is presented without assurance regarding its prolonged validity or interim quality. Mention of trademarks is done without written consent and should not be construed as an endorsement from the trademark holder.

TABLE OF CONTENTS

INTRODUCTION 9
THE PHILOSOPHY OF DR. BARBARA O'NEILL 9
- UNDERSTANDING THE BODY'S HEALING MECHANISMS 9
- THE ROLE OF NUTRITION IN HEALING 11
- THE IMPORTANCE OF DETOXIFICATION 13
- MIND-BODY CONNECTION 15
- THE POWER OF WHOLE FOODS 17
- SUSTAINABLE HEALTH PRACTICES 19

YOUR 365-DAY JOURNEY TO BETTER HEALTH 21
- SETTING HEALTH GOALS 21
- DAILY HEALTH PRACTICES 23
- STAYING MOTIVATED AND COMMITTED 25

UNDERSTANDING YOUR BODY'S NEEDS 27
- NUTRITIONAL REQUIREMENTS 27
- LISTENING TO YOUR BODY 30
- SPECIAL DIETARY CONSIDERATIONS 33
- ENHANCING DIGESTIVE HEALTH 35

2. BREAKFAST 37
- Omega Power Smoothie Bowl 37
- Anti-Inflammatory Turmeric Oatmeal 37
- Turmeric Ginger Oatmeal 38
- Quinoa & Blueberry Breakfast Porridge 39
- Quinoa & Spinach Breakfast Muffins 40
- Ginger Pear Oatmeal 41
- Quinoa & Spinach Power Breakfast 41
- Quinoa & Spinach Power Breakfast Bowl 42
- Spiced Quinoa & Chia Breakfast Bowl 43

3. SOUPS 45
- Healing Ginger-Turmeric Carrot Soup 45

Ginger-Spiced Pumpkin Soup 46

Healing Turmeric Ginger Soup 47

Gingered Butternut Squash Soup 47

Healing Ginger Carrot Soup 48

Healing Ginger-Pumpkin Soup 49

Soothing Ginger Turmeric Soup 50

Healing Turmeric Lentil Soup 51

Healing Ginger Pumpkin Soup 52

4. MAIN DISH 55

Quinoa & Black Bean Stuffed Peppers 55

Zesty Lemon Herb Chicken 56

Quinoa & Roasted Vegetable Bowl 57

Lemon Garlic Roasted Chicken with Root Vegetables 58

Quinoa Stuffed Bell Peppers 59

Turmeric-Spiced Quinoa with Roasted Vegetables 60

Quinoa and Roasted Vegetable Bowl 61

5. SNACK RECIPES 63

Spiced Chickpea Crunch 63

Spiced Roasted Chickpeas 63

Spicy Avocado and Chickpea Toast 64

Spicy Avocado Hummus 65

Zesty Avocado and Chickpea Hummus 66

Spiced Roasted Chickpeas 67

6. DINNER 69

Mediterranean Stuffed Bell Peppers 69

Ginger-Soy Glazed Salmon with Broccoli 70

Lemon Garlic Roasted Chicken with Asparagus 71

Ginger-Lime Baked Salmon with Asparagus 72

Turmeric-Ginger Grilled Chicken 72

Lemon-Herb Grilled Salmon with Asparagus 73

Grilled Polenta with Ratatouille 74

Zesty Lemon Herb Chicken with Asparagus 75

7. DESSERT 77

Coconut Chia Almond Delight 77

Avocado Lime Cheesecake 77

No-Bake Coconut Cashew Bars 79

Spiced Avocado Chocolate Mousse 79

Zesty Orange and Almond Flour Cake 80

Almond and Coconut Flour Berry Crisp 81

8. HEALTH SMOOTHIE 83

Green Goddess Detox Smoothie 83

Vibrant Greens Detox Smoothie 83

Anti-Inflammatory Berry Bliss Smoothie 84

Anti-Inflammatory Berry Spice Smoothie 85

Green Detox Power Smoothie 86

28 DAYS MEAL PLAN 89

9. BASICS HOLISTIC HEALING MEDICINE 93

INTRODUCTION TO HOLISTIC MEDICINE 93

NATURAL REMEDIES AND TREATMENTS 96

MIND-BODY CONNECTION 99

INTEGRATING HOLISTIC PRACTICES INTO DAILY LIFE 102

10. CONCLUSION 105

MEASUREMENT CONVERSION TABLE 107

INTRODUCTION
THE PHILOSOPHY OF DR. BARBARA O'NEILL

UNDERSTANDING THE BODY'S HEALING MECHANISMS

In the treasure trove of holistic health, understanding the body's inherent ability to heal itself is akin to discovering the first clue on a map to long-term wellness. Dr. Barbara O'Neill, a beacon in the field of natural health, offers a profound perspective on the philosophy underlying our body's healing capabilities. The essence of her philosophy is simple yet revolutionary: given the right conditions and sustenance, the human body can restore its own health and fend off ailments effectively and naturally.

Imagine your body as a complex, highly efficient ecosystem. Every part, from the smallest cell to the largest organ, is designed to work harmoniously and respond adaptively to internal and external cues. When you scrape your knee, blood clots form swiftly; if you catch a cold, your immune system kicks into high gear to fight off the virus. These everyday healing events share a common ground—they begin and end with the body's intrinsic wisdom.

Dr. O'Neill's insights deepen as we explore the cellular level of healing. Every cell in our body is a powerhouse of recovery. It's equipped with mechanisms to repair DNA, regenerate itself, and communicate with other cells to maintain overall health. When you consume a nutrient-rich diet, you are not merely eating for energy; you are providing your cells with the tools they need to perform these vital functions efficiently.

Detoxification is another cornerstone of our body's self-healing. Our organs, especially the liver and kidneys, are constantly at work, removing toxins from our bodies. Imagine this process as a complex dance, where each step needs to be executed perfectly to keep the performance seamless. When we support these organs with a clean diet and adequate hydration, we ensure that the dance continues without a misstep, aiding in our overall health resilience.

Moreover, the connection between the brain and the rest of the body cannot be overstated in its role in healing. Our thoughts and emotions significantly impact our physical health. If you are continuously stressed, your body releases more of the hormone cortisol, which can impede healing. On the other hand, positive emotions can enhance your body's healing capabilities by boosting the immune function and reducing pain. Dr. O'Neill encourages the cultivation of a positive mindset as part of the healing journey. Nutrition plays a pivotal role in our healing processes. Every bite we take can either support or hinder our health. Foods high in antioxidants, for instance, combat oxidative stress—a condition that can damage cells and hinder healing. By choosing whole foods over processed ones, we feed our bodies the best fuel to promote recovery and health. It's like choosing high-quality lumber to build a house. The better the materials, the sturdier the home.

Incorporating sustainable health practices is also vital. This includes not just what we eat but how we live. Regular physical activity, adequate sleep, and stress management are all parts of a holistic approach to health that supports the body's natural healing abilities. Each element is crucial; neglecting one can throw off the balance, much like skipping a crucial ingredient in a recipe can spoil a dish.

Understanding your body and its signals is a skill that comes with patience and attention. Dr. O'Neill emphasizes the importance of listening to our body's cues. Are you feeling fatigued? Perhaps your body is telling you to take a step back and rest. Are you experiencing persistent discomfort? It might be a signal to examine your diet or reduce stress. Tuning in to these messages allows us to make informed choices about our health.

Special dietary considerations also play a role in tailoring the healing journey to individual needs. Each person's body is unique, with different susceptibilities and nutritional requirements. What works for one might not work for another. This personalized approach is akin to designing a custom suit—it must fit perfectly to function properly. Finally, enhancing digestive health is crucial for effective healing. The gut is often referred to as the 'second brain' for its significant impact on overall health and its ability to communicate with the brain via the gut-brain axis. A healthy gut contributes to a strong immune system, effective detoxification, and efficient nutrient absorption—all essential to healing.

Dr. Barbara O'Neill's philosophy isn't just about treating or even preventing disease; it's about creating an environment within your body that promotes optimal health and effortless healing. It's about making daily choices that align with the profound respect for the intricacies of our biological systems.

THE ROLE OF NUTRITION IN HEALING

There is an ancient saying that suggests, "Let food be thy medicine and medicine be thy food," a maxim that captures the linchpin role nutrition holds within the philosophy of natural healing championed by Dr. Barbara O'Neill. This approach not only anchors her ethos but is also a guiding star for those seeking to mend and fortify their bodies through the natural bounty of the earth.

The concept of food as medicine isn't a fleeting trend but rather a return to the basics—understanding that what we put into our bodies fundamentally shapes our health outcomes. Dr. O'Neill enlightens her wisdom upon us, showing how specific nutrients and foods can act not just as sustenance, but as powerful agents of healing and prevention.

Take, for example, inflammation, the body's natural response to injury or attack by viruses or bacteria. While acute inflammation is beneficial—protecting and healing the body—chronic inflammation can lead to a myriad of health issues. The right dietary choices can significantly douse the flames of chronic inflammation. Foods rich in omega-3 fatty acids, like flaxseeds and walnuts, have been shown to help reduce the body's inflammatory responses, effectively supporting the healing process.

Let us consider the path of a nutrient as it enters the body, a fascinating journey from consumption to assimilation. Picture the humble spinach leaf—rich in iron, fiber, and essential vitamins. When consumed, these components travel through the digestive system, each finding its way to specific functions and cellular processes that aid in repairing, fortifying, and energizing the body. Iron helps in the formation of hemoglobin, which transports oxygen to our cells, invigorating our entire system—an elementary yet profound cascade of healing starting from a single leaf.

Dr. O'Neill also puts a spotlight on the gut, often termed the second brain due to its crucial role in overall health and wellness. A healthy gut populated with beneficial bacteria is key to efficient digestion, absorption of nutrients, and even the production of certain vitamins. By nurturing our gut health through prebiotics and probiotics found naturally in foods such as yogurt, kefir, and certain whole grains, we bolster our body's healing forces.

The synergy between nutrients also plays a critical role. Some nutrients, when consumed together, dramatically improve each other's absorption rates and effectiveness. The classic example is the combination of vitamin C and iron. Found separately in citrus fruits and leafy greens, when eaten together, vitamin C enhances iron absorption, multiplying the benefits, and better fortifying the body's iron supplies, thereby intensifying its healing capacity. This nutritional journey transcends merely choosing the right types of food; it includes understanding the timing and combinations that maximize the body's uptake and use of these vital substances. Dr. O'Neill advocates for mindful eating—being fully present with our food, understanding where it comes from, how it affects our bodies, and how best to combine it for optimal benefits. However, embracing nutrition as a cornerstone of healing is not without its challenges. Modern lifestyles often lead to hurried meals, processed foods, and neglected micronutrients. Dr. O'Neill encourages a return to whole, unprocessed foods, which naturally contain the spectrum of nutrients our bodies require. She reminds us that each meal is an opportunity to support our health, urging us to make choices that are in harmony with our body's needs. Furthermore, the concept of bio-individuality—the understanding that no single diet works for everyone—is central to Dr. O'Neill's teachings.

Each person's body is unique with individual nutritional needs based on factors like age, health, activity level, and genetic predispositions. By embracing a diet tailored to personal needs, one embarks on a more effective, more personal healing journey.

Detoxification, another crucial aspect of healing, greatly benefits from proper nutrition. Certain foods, such as beets, garlic, and green tea, are known for their detoxifying properties, helping the body rid itself of harmful toxins and enhancing its natural healing processes. In this narrative of nutrition and healing, every food choice becomes a profound decision—a step towards health or away from it. Dr. O'Neill's philosophy empowers us, turning daily meals into deliberate acts of nurturing. She doesn't just offer a diet plan; she provides a roadmap to a vibrant, healthful life, encouraging everyone to make thoughtful, informed choices about what they eat.

THE IMPORTANCE OF DETOXIFICATION

Consider our body as a complex, sophisticated piece of machinery. Over time, just like any machine, it can accumulate 'waste' - not just physical but biochemical and emotional. The build-up of toxins from processed foods, polluted environments, stress, and unmetabolized emotions can clog the pathways that nourish life into our cells and organs, dampening the body's innate ability to heal. Detoxification then becomes crucial, acting almost like a 'reset button,' allowing the body to rid itself of these impurities and restore natural health rhythms.

Dr. O'Neill emphasizes that detoxification is not a one-time event but a dynamic, ongoing process. It involves supporting the body's own systems specifically designed for this purpose—the liver, kidneys, lungs, skin, and lymphatic system. Each plays a critical role in filtering out toxins that, if accumulated, could disrupt bodily functions and lead to illness.

The liver, often hailed as the body's primary detox organ, processes everything from old blood cells to chemicals in food. Imagine the liver as a meticulous sorter, distinguishing between nutrients to absorb and toxins to discard. Aiding the liver with foods rich in antioxidants such as leafy greens and berries, can enhance its function, propelling the clearance of toxins more efficiently.

Next, consider the kidneys, vital organs that filter waste from the blood. They work in tandem with the liver, converting toxins into forms that can be easily eliminated through urine. Hydration plays a fundamental role here—water not only transports nutrients to various parts of the body but also helps flush out toxins. The simple act of drinking sufficient water becomes an act of cleansing, promoting the kidneys' filtration work.

The lungs, too, participate actively in detoxification. Each breath expels carbon dioxide—a metabolic waste—cleansing the body continuously. Pathways such as deep breathing exercises enhance lung capacity and efficiency, aiding in better expulsion of toxins.

Our skin, which is our largest organ, detoxifies through sweat. Regular physical activity and sauna sessions can promote sweating, a process through which the body expels toxins, including heavy metals like lead and mercury.

Lastly, the often-overlooked lymphatic system, working quietly alongside our circulatory system, carries out the important task of transporting waste away from tissues and into the bloodstream to be processed for elimination. Physical activities, especially those that stimulate movement and balance, like yoga or tai chi, support lymphatic circulation and help keep the detox pathways open.

As much as detoxification involves the physical body, Dr. O'Neill reminds us of the mental and emotional components. Emotional detox, though less visible, is just as critical. Unprocessed emotions can linger, metaphorically 'toxifying' our mental state. Practices such as meditation, journaling, and therapy can be essential tools for emotional detoxification, helping clear out mental clutter that can manifest as physical ailments. Detoxification also calls for a mindful consideration of what we expose ourselves to. This includes the quality of food, the air we breathe, the water we drink, and even the relationships and environments we engage with. Each choice has a profound impact on our body's toxic burden.

While detox diets and cleanses are popular, Dr. O'Neill focuses on the importance of a sustained, holistic approach to detoxification. Rather than periodic intense detoxes, she advocates for incorporating detox-friendly practices and foods into daily life. This sustainable approach not only supports detoxification but also strengthens the body's own defenses over time. Understanding and implementing effective detoxification under Dr. O'Neill's guidance is akin to gardening; it's about removing the weeds and debris (toxins) while nurturing the soil (our body) so that it can support healthy plants (cells and organs) that bear beautiful flowers and fruits (optimal health). Embracing this comprehensive approach transforms our perspective on detoxification—from a periodic cleanse to a continuous, mindful effort towards health. It carves a path towards not just surviving, but thriving, with clarity, vitality, and resilience.

MIND-BODY CONNECTION

In the holistic vista of health that Dr. Barbara O'Neill paints, the mind-body connection is not just an abstract concept but a vibrant, pulsating reality that affects every aspect of our being. Delving into this interconnectedness unveils a powerful alliance between mental states and physical health, reminding us that healing and wellness encompass far more than just the physical body.

Imagine your body as a garden and your mind as the sunlight it needs to flourish. The quality of thoughts can rain down nurture or neglect, determining the vitality and bloom of the garden. Dr. O'Neill emphasizes that positive mental and emotional health are not just beneficial but essential for achieving physical health. Stress, anxiety, and negativity act like shadows that stifle growth, while positivity and peace are like rays of sunlight, promoting growth and renewal.

Let's navigate through the science behind this phenomenon. Neurotransmitters, the chemical messengers of our bodies, are directly influenced by our mental states. Serotonin, often dubbed the 'happiness hormone,' plays a significant role in this linkage. Originating largely from our gastrointestinal tract—often influenced by the foods we eat—serotonin levels are directly tied to our sense of well-being. High levels of serotonin boost our mood, enhance our immune system, and even aid in digestion. Herein lies a clear example of how the gut and brain, though physically apart, communicate intimately through the biochemical language, influencing our overall health.

Our cardiac system also tells a tale of this deep connection. The heart is not just a pump but an emotional organ that can be profoundly affected by our thoughts and feelings. Research has shown that a positive emotional state can lead to a decrease in blood pressure, reduced risk of heart disease, and overall better heart health. Conversely, negative emotions can lead to an increase in stress hormones like cortisol, which constrict blood vessels and reduce blood flow, eventually leading into deteriorative cardiac conditions.

Then there's the immune system, our body's defense mechanism which is significantly modulated by our psychological state. Positive thinking can act almost like a vaccine, bolstering the immune response to face off illnesses. For instance, an optimistic outlook has been linked with better cellular immunity; the opposite can happen with persistent sadness or depression, which can weaken the body's immune responses to pathogens. Beyond mere physiology, Dr. O'Neill promotes practices that nurture the mind-body connection to harness this power for healing. Meditation, mindfulness, and yoga are not just trends but ancient practices that modern science supports for their benefits in synchronizing the mind and body. Regular meditation, for instance, can modify the neural pathways in the brain, making you more resilient to stress and thus indirectly but beneficially affecting physical health. Also central in Dr. O'Neill's approach is the concept of emotional release.

Like toxins that can build up in the physical body, emotional blockages can hinder mental and physical health. Techniques such as deep breathing exercises, guided imagery, or even expressive writing can facilitate an emotional detox that can be as crucial as a physical cleanse.

Environmental influences also play a part in the mind-body dialogue. Surroundings that promote peace and provide sensory pleasure—like natural settings, soothing sounds, or comforting aromas—can drastically improve mental and emotional health, which in turn reflects in physical wellness. Dr. O'Neill encourages creating and seeking spaces that provide these sensory inputs to reinforce the mind-body bridge.

Lastly, fostering relationships that encourage positive interactions can create environments that enhance the mind-body connection. Social interactions can stimulate our brain in positive ways, influencing our mental and physical health through complex psychosocial mechanisms. Dr. O'Neill enjoins us to view our health as a holistic integration wherein the mind and body are inseparable allies, each influencing the other continuously. By caring for the mind, we are, in a very real sense, caring for the body. This integrated approach not only helps in addressing immediate health concerns but also in preventing future ailments, crafting a vibrant tapestry. Understanding and implementing the mind-body connection as illuminated by Dr. O'Neill can transform the way we perceive health and healing. It's akin to learning a new language—the language of our own body and mind—that once mastered, opens up a new realm of wellness and vitality that is comprehensive and enduring.

THE POWER OF WHOLE FOODS

The celebration of whole foods begins with an appreciation of their complete form—their untouched, unprocessed state. Imagine a bright orange, plucked from a lush tree, brimming with vitamin C, fibers, and more than one hundred other phytochemicals in their natural ratios. Compare this to a bottle of commercial vitamin C—the isolation changes the context, and the synergy of combined nutrients found in the whole fruit enhances nutrient absorption and provides additional health benefits like improved skin health and immune support.

Dr. O'Neill often emphasizes that whole foods are infused with nature's wisdom. They inherently contain a balance of nutrients that work together to nourish and heal the body effectively. It's akin to receiving a gift that's perfectly wrapped and exactly what you need—there's no need to unwrap or dissect it further. The body recognizes these foods, knows how to break them down, and how to use their components optimally.

Take, for example, the humble oat. It's a powerhouse of nutrition, offering layers of benefits from its complex carbohydrates, fiber, vitamins, and minerals—in particular, the beta-glucan found in oats has been shown to help regulate cholesterol levels and boost heart health. Consumed in its whole form, it retains all its natural fiber and nutrients which aids in digestion and sustained energy release.

Further, the integration of whole foods supports not only individual health but also the health of the planet. Processing foods often require significant energy and resources and can contribute to waste and environmental degradation. Choosing whole foods reduces this burden, placing us in a harmonious relationship with the environment—a concept deeply rooted in Dr. O'Neill's teachings about sustainable health practices.

Another aspect underlining the power of whole foods is their diversity. The array of vegetables, fruits, grains, nuts, seeds, and legumes available offers a plethora of nutritional benefits—colors, textures, and flavors can all be tailored to meet dietary needs and preferences, making it an exciting exploration of taste and health benefits. Each color in fruits and vegetables represents different antioxidants and phytochemicals that protect the body against diseases. Eating a "rainbow" of whole foods, therefore, naturally ensures a comprehensive intake of these vital nutrients. Dr. O'Neill also addresses the glycemic impact of foods. Whole foods generally have lower glycemic indices and therefore provide a more stable energy release, which helps maintain insulin levels and prevents spikes in blood sugar. For example, the natural fruit sugars in an apple, combined with its fiber, are digested slower than the refined sugars, helping to maintain energy levels and satiety for longer.

In addressing the modern challenges of diet, it becomes clear how distant many have strayed from natural eating habits. Processed and fast foods dominate for their convenience, but they lack many of the benefits whole foods provide. Adopting a diet rich in whole foods may require a shift in routine and mindset, but it is a fundamental step back towards optimal health.

Moreover, Dr. O'Neill advises that transitioning to a whole food diet be a gradual process, encouraging individuals to make small, manageable changes rather than abrupt shifts. Perhaps start with integrating more fresh fruits and vegetables, replacing refined grains with whole grains, and choosing unprocessed protein sources. This not only uplifts physical health but also enhances overall vitality and quality of life. Through Dr. O'Neill's teachings, it becomes evident that embracing whole foods is far more than a dietary choice—it's a commitment to a life-enriching philosophy that advocates for a return to nature's basics. It's about reestablishing a profound connection with the foods we eat and, by extension, the earth we inhabit. This holistic approach does not merely chase symptoms but nurtures the root itself, encouraging a full bloom of health that is visible in the clarity of the skin, the vitality of movement, and the joy of overall well-being. In this light, whole foods become not just a dietary element, but powerful symbols of life's energy and healing potential.

SUSTAINABLE HEALTH PRACTICES

Imagine sustainability as a tree. Its roots ground in personal health practices, the trunk symbolizes the community, and the branches reach out to the environmental impacts of our choices. This interconnected structure illustrates how our personal health practices affect broader ecological and societal systems and vice versa.

At the root of sustainable health is the choice of diet. Dr. O'Neill encourages a diet primarily composed of whole, plant-based foods. These choices are not only nourishing at a bodily level but they are also less taxing on the environment compared to diets high in animal-based products. Agriculture focused on plant production emits lower levels of greenhouse gases, uses fewer resources, and can be more sustainably managed.

Moving up to the trunk, community involvement is vital. This includes supporting local farmers and producers which not only reduces the carbon footprint associated with long transportation routes but also helps to sustain the local economy. Participating in local food co-ops or community-supported agriculture (CSC)s can connect individuals to their food sources, fostering a connection with the land and the origin of their nourishment.

Branching out, sustainable health practices also prioritize reducing waste. This includes minimizing consumption of single-use plastics and disposables in the kitchen by opting for alternatives like beeswax wraps, reusable containers, and cloth bags. Composting organic waste is another practice Dr. O'Neill supports; it not only reduces landfill contribution but also returns nutrients to the earth, promoting soil health and reducing the need for chemical fertilizers.

Another critical aspect is the use of clean, renewable energy sources where possible. For instance, using solar panels can reduce reliance on fossil fuels and decrease the ecological footprint of an individual or household. Moreover, energy efficiency in the home — through insulation, LED lighting, and energy-efficient appliances — not only reduces environmental impact but also saves money, proving that sustainability can be economically favorable as well. Dr. O'Neill also espouses the sustainable practice of water conservation. Simple adjustments like fixing leaks, installing low-flow fixtures, and using greywater systems can significantly reduce water usage. In the garden, choosing native plants that require less water than non-native species can further contribute to a sustainable lifestyle. Incorporating physical activity into daily routines is another pillar of Dr. O'Neill's sustainable health practices. Whether it's biking to work, gardening, or practicing yoga at home, regular physical activity not only improves physical health but also reduces the need for motor vehicle transport, thereby contributing to cleaner air and reduced greenhouse gas emissions. Mindful meditation and stress management are also integral to sustainable health.

By maintaining a balanced state of mind through practices like meditation, individuals can manage stress more effectively. This psychological wellbeing is crucial as chronic stress can lead to a host of health issues, which in turn increases healthcare usage and its associated environmental footprint.

Education plays a foundational role in sustainable health practices. Being informed about the impacts of our choices allows us to make better decisions. Dr. O'Neill advocates for ongoing learning about nutrition, the environment, and wellness strategies. This education can empower individuals to make choices that are grounded in knowledge, not just habit or convenience. Balancing these practices requires an appreciation of their interconnectivity and the effects they have not only on personal health but also on societal well-being and environmental health. Dr. O'Neill's sustainable health practices are not merely about sustaining good health over time; they are about nourished living that supports a vibrant life for oneself and the planet. Indeed, adopting sustainable health practices as guided by Dr. O'Neill can be likened to nurturing a garden. It takes care, effort, and consistency, but the harvest is rich—a flourishing of personal health, a resilient community, and a thriving environment. By embracing these practices, each person contributes to a legacy of health and sustainability that benefits current and future generations.

YOUR 365-DAY JOURNEY TO BETTER HEALTH
SETTING HEALTH GOALS

Imagine standing at the base of a stunning, yet daunting mountain. You aim to reach the summit, to overlook worlds beyond your own. The journey up this mountain does not start with your first step on the trail; it begins with charting your route, understanding the terrain, assessing the weather, and preparing your supplies. In setting health goals, a similar approach is essential. Instead of a physical map and compass, you're equipped with knowledge, self-awareness, and a tailored plan that suits your body's unique landscape.

Understanding the Importance of Tailored Goals

Each individual's body, lifestyle, and responsibilities are different. What works remarkably well for one may not suit another. This underscores the importance of setting personalized health goals. Sara, a mother of two, found herself struggling with fatigue and chronic inflammation. For years, she juggled her roles, neglecting her own health needs. When Sara finally decided to prioritize her health, her first step was to seek understanding of her own body's responses to certain foods and stress. Her journey began not with radical changes, but with establishing small, manageable goals that addressed her specific conditions.

Crafting Realistic and Achievable Objectives

When defining your goals, lean towards those that are realistic and measurable. For example, rather than a vague aim like "eat healthier," specify what this looks like daily or weekly. It could be "incorporate two servings of leafy greens into my diet per day" or "prepare home-cooked meals five times a week." These particular activities are not only actionable but also allow you to track your progress clearly. In setting these goals, remember to consider your current lifestyle, the demands of your professional work, your family commitments, and your personal capacity. Incremental changes often lead to sustainable habits. Goals should stretch you, but not to the point of breaking. They should challenge yet be achievable, providing a sense of victory and encouragement with each step forward.

Integrating Goals into Daily Life

A perennial challenge in sustaining new health practices is in their seamless integration into everyday life. How do you make these goals a natural part of your day-to-day rhythm? Integration can be facilitated through routine. For instance, if part of your health goal is to engage more in physical activity, consider routine processes such as taking a brisk walk after lunch each day or participating in a yoga class twice a week. Incorporating these activities within established daily patterns increases the likelihood of adherence and success.

Lucas, a software developer, discovered that his sedentary job contributed to his weight gain and discomfort. By scheduling regular intervals during his workday designated for short walks or stretching, he not only improved his physical wellbeing but also his productivity and mental clarity.

Monitoring and Adjusting Your Goals

One aspect almost as crucial as setting goals is the regular monitoring and adjusting of these goals. Keeping a health diary or using a digital app to track your progress can be profoundly enlightening. Tracking allows you to celebrate successes, understand pitfalls, and see the tangible results of your hard work. It also provides crucial insights into what adjustments might be necessary to better align with your evolving needs or changing circumstances.

Ellen, for instance, noticed through her monthly health tracking that she struggled to meet her hydration goals consistently. With this insight, she adjusted her goal to include carrying a reusable water bottle, which significantly increased her daily water intake.

Celebrating Milestones

Setting milestones within your larger goal framework can provide additional motivation and joy in your journey. Whether it's treating yourself to a new book or a relaxing spa day after achieving a month of your dietary goals, these celebrations can act as both acknowledgments of your hard work and incentives to maintain your momentum.

The Power of Community in Goal Achievement

Lastly, remember the power of community. Sharing your goals with a friend, family member, or online group can foster a sense of support and accountability. Maya found that by joining a local vegetarian group, she not only gained new recipes that fit her goals but also formed friendships that made her nutritional journey enjoyable and sustainable.

As you set forth on your 365-day journey to better health, remember that the process of setting health goals is not just about marking checklists; it's about creating a vision for your life that values health and wellbeing. Your goals are the maps and tools, your determination the vehicle. With these in hand, each step forward is a step towards a more vibrant, fulfilling life.

DAILY HEALTH PRACTICES

Picture this: every morning, you wake to the gentle sunlight filtering through your curtains and your first action is a deep, cleansing breath followed by a moment of gratitude. This simple morning ritual sets the tone for the day, ensuring that you begin with a calm, centered mind. Such is the power of daily health practices—they instill a sense of rhythm and purpose that guides you through the challenges of each day.

The Pivotal Morning Routine

Imagine Jenny, a busy graphic designer and a mother of two, who found herself overwhelmed each morning, scrambling to get her kids ready for school, barely having time to sip her coffee. She decided to wake up 30 minutes earlier each day to practice yoga and meditation. This slight adjustment not only provided her with a quiet time to focus on herself but also left her energized and more present with her children. Her mornings transformed from chaotic to peaceful, profoundly affecting her overall day and health.

Incorporating Mindful Eating

As the day progresses, one's focus often shifts to meals—breakfast, lunch, and dinner. Mindful eating is a practice which involves paying full attention to the experience of eating and drinking. It's about noticing the colors, smells, textures, and flavors of your food, about chewing slowly and relishing each bite. When people eat mindfully, they often find that they eat less but feel more satisfied because they are truly savoring the meal.

Consider Mark, who had the habit of eating lunch at his desk, often finishing his food without even tasting it. After learning about mindful eating, he began to schedule a dedicated block of time for lunch away from his workspace. This small change helped him enjoy his food, improved his digestion, and reduced his usual mid-afternoon slump.

The Importance of Physical Activity

Physical activity is another cornerstone of daily health practices. It doesn't necessarily imply rigorous gym sessions. What is vital is consistency and enjoyment in the activity chosen. Whether it's a 15-minute morning stretch, a 30-minute home workout session, or an evening walk with your dog, the goal is to move your body regularly. Clara, an author, incorporated brief dance breaks into her writing routine. Every hour, she would put on her favorite song and dance around her living room for a few minutes.

This not only improved her physical stamina but also boosted her creativity and writing.

Hydration and Its Myriad Benefits

Drinking adequate water is another simple yet effective practice for maintaining health. Water supports metabolism, skin health, and digestion, among other vital functions. Carrying a water bottle and setting reminders to drink can be beneficial strategies for those often forgetting to hydrate. Ben, a software engineer, realized he was chronically dehydrated when he started logging his water intake. By setting hourly reminders, he gradually increased his water intake, which dramatically improved his energy levels and decreased his daily headaches.

Connection and Reflection: Evening Practices

As important as how you start your day is how you end it. Evening routines are crucial in signaling to your body that it's time to wind down and prepare for rest. Practices might include writing in a gratitude journal, reading a book, turning off electronic devices an hour before bed, or practicing gentle stretches or deep breathing exercises.

Emma, a nurse, found that her stress levels were significantly high after her shifts. She incorporated an evening routine of herbal tea and journaling which helped her transition from her workday into a peaceful sleep, reducing her insomnia and anxiety.

Regular Health Checks and Adjustments

Incorporating regular check-ins on your own progress can help recalibrate your daily practices as needed. Health isn't static; it's dynamic and responsive to changes in your environment, stress levels, and body. What works one month might need adjustment the next.

Sophie, inspired by periodic self-review sessions, tweaked her diet to include more iron-rich foods after noticing her energy levels were low. This small dietary change had a profound impact on her overall vitality and motivation. These stories underscore that health is not merely the absence of disease; it's a vibrant state of wellbeing that's nurtured day by day, through the small but significant choices we make from morning to night. Through consistent daily practices, you not only create a life that feels good but one that fundamentally supports your long-term health and happiness on this 365-day journey and beyond.

Staying Motivated and Committed

Discovering Your 'Why'

Consider Linda, a high school teacher with diabetes. Her turning point came during a casual chat with her grandchildren about future family vacations—vacations she feared she might not be around to experience if she continued neglecting her health. That very moment ignited a fierce determination in Linda. Her 'why' was clear and potent. She wanted to improve her health not just for herself but to be part of her grandchildren's future adventures. Understanding the deep-seated reasons behind your health goals is instrumental. It's not solely about losing weight, managing a health condition, or looking good. It's often more about living life to the fullest, fulfilling dreams, nurturing relationships, and being able to participate actively in your own life and the lives of those you love.

Setting Small, Measurable Goals

Big dreams start with small, realistic steps. When goals are overly ambitious, they can feel daunting and may lead to discouragement. Breaking them down into smaller, manageable tasks can keep the journey enjoyable and less overwhelming. Each small success builds confidence and momentum, making the next step feel attainable. John, a freelance writer, wanted to reduce his cholesterol levels without medication. He started by incorporating a 10-minute walk into his daily routine. Over time, this walk became a 30-minute jog, and he started experimenting with heart-healthy recipes. John didn't transform his lifestyle overnight, but he progressed steadily, motivated by each small victory.

Leveraging Support Systems

Journeying alone can be tough and lonely. Having a support system in place can provide encouragement, share in your struggles, and celebrate your successes. This could be a formal arrangement like a fitness class or a health coach, or an informal one like a group of friends or a community online. Emma tapped into online forums where others shared their struggles with hypertension. Through her interactions, she got not only practical advice but also emotional support that reminded her she wasn't alone in her challenges.

Keeping the Journey Interesting

Variety, they say, is the spice of life, and it holds true for maintaining motivation in health routines. Sticking rigidly to a specific workout, meal plan, or daily routine can lead to boredom. Introducing new activities, recipes, and practices can keep excitement alive and prevent burnout. Laura, for instance, loved her weekly yoga but decided to spice things up by adding salsa dancing classes to her routine. Not only did she find a new passion, but she also met new friends, which doubled her enthusiasm for her broader health goals.

Revisiting and Adjusting Goals Regularly

What happens when you hit a plateau, face unexpected challenges, or find your circumstances have changed? Staying rigid can lead to frustration and demotivation. The key is flexibility—revisiting your goals and adjusting them as needed. This adaptive approach ensures that your health journey stays relevant and aligned with your life.

For Mike, an initial weight loss goal was quickly achieved, leading to lost motivation post-goal. By reassessing his aims, he set himself new challenges like building muscle and improving his endurance, which reinvigorated his commitment.

Celebrating Progress

Never underestimate the power of celebrating milestones, no matter how small. These celebrations reinforce positive behavior and keep the flame of motivation burning. Whether it's treating yourself to a massage after a month of clean eating or a small weekend getaway after six months of consistent gym attendance, acknowledging your hard work is crucial. Zoe celebrated every five pounds she lost by buying a charm for her bracelet, a visible reminder of her progress and a personal symbol of her commitment to her health.

Embracing Setbacks as Part of the Journey

Lastly, it is crucial to acknowledge that setbacks are an inevitable part of any journey. The path to health is not linear. It zigs and zags, moves up and down. Embracing setbacks as learning opportunities rather than failures can refocus and refine your strategy, making your health goals even more resilient. When Tom suffered a knee injury, his initial reaction was despair; his marathon training came to an abrupt halt. However, during his recovery, he discovered swimming, which not only became part of his cross-training but also a new passion. These narratives underline that staying motivated and remaining committed requires understanding your deeper motivations, setting reasonable goals, building a supportive environment, adding variety, appreciating your progress, and being adaptable to changes and setbacks. Uniting all these elements helps keep the journey towards health not just ongoing but also fulfilling and enriching.

UNDERSTANDING YOUR BODY'S NEEDS

NUTRITIONAL REQUIREMENTS

Understanding the nutritional needs of our bodies can often feel like navigating a maze with multiple paths, each claiming to be the definitive route to health. Yet, the journey towards achieving optimal health through nutrition need not be complex when approached thoughtfully and informed by reliable knowledge. Drawing inspiration from Dr. Barbara O'Neill's philosophically rich approach to wellness, we delve deeply into how our nutritional requirements are not only foundational to maintaining health but essential in healing and preventing ailments. Nutrition is much more than the act of eating; it's the art of nourishing our bodies and nurturing our souls. It is essential to recognize that each individual's nutritional needs are unique—a beautiful diversity reflected in the array of diets and practices that different cultures and individuals uphold around the world. This diversity signals the need for a personalized approach to nutrition that respects our individual bodies, lifestyles, and health statuses.

At its core, good nutrition revolves around understanding and supplying the nutrients that are critical for the body's functions: carbohydrates for energy, proteins for repair and growth, fats for long-term energy and cell health, vitamins, and minerals for various biochemical processes. Water, often overlooked, is crucial in this matrix as it facilitates digestion, absorption, and transport of nutrients, alongside its role in temperature regulation and cellular homeostasis.

The Importance of Macronutrients and Micronutrients

Carbohydrates, fats, and proteins form the cornerstone of our dietary needs—collectively known as macronutrients, they supply the energy necessary to sustain daily activities. However, the modern dietary landscape often distorts these needs, leading to an overconsumption of processed carbs and unhealthy fats, casting a shadow over the equally important consumption of high-quality proteins and fats from natural sources like nuts, seeds, fish, and avocados. Including a balance of these macronutrients is not only vital for energy but essential in managing weight, supporting metabolic health, and reducing inflammation.

Beyond energy, our bodies crave micronutrients—vitamins and minerals—which, though required in smaller amounts, are potent forces in health maintenance. These mighty molecules support the immune system, aid in the repair of DNA, and play roles in countless enzymatic reactions vital to life. Whether it's the antioxidant properties of vitamins A, C, and E, protecting our cells against oxidative stress, or the bone-strengthening duo of calcium and vitamin D, each micronutrient is a hero in its right.

Listening and Responding to Your Body's Signals

Our bodies communicate continuously through signals such as energy levels, digestion, skin health, and more. For instance, frequent fatigue could signal inadequate iron intake, particularly in women, or a lack of sufficient quality sleep might suggest poor magnesium intake. Learning to listen and interpret these signals is a profound step toward understanding and meeting your nutritional needs.

The Role of Diet in Managing and Preventing Disease

The connection between diet and disease is incontrovertible in the scientific literature. Diets rich in processed foods and sugars contribute to the prevalence of diabetes, heart disease, and obesity. Conversely, diets abundant in whole foods, rich in fiber, healthy fats, and lean proteins can help manage, mitigate, or even prevent these conditions. Particularly in the context of inflammation—a root cause of many chronic diseases—a diet focused on anti-inflammatory foods, like berries, green leafy vegetables, and fatty fish, can significantly affect health outcomes.

Transitioning to such a diet isn't merely about choosing different foods; it's about initiating a deeper change in how we relate to food. It involves recognizing food as medicine, understanding that every bite we take can either support our health or contribute to disease.

Synthesizing a Nutritional Plan That Works for You

Creating a nutritional plan shouldn't feel restrictive or burdensome—it should be a liberating experience that enlightens numerous possibilities for healing and wellness. Begin with small, manageable changes. Swap out processed snack foods with whole fruit, incorporate a salad at lunch daily, choose whole grains over refined ones — these small choices accumulate to create substantial positive impacts over time.

Moreover, consider your lifestyle and any specific health conditions which might require adjustments in your diet. Work with healthcare providers or nutritionists who appreciate the holistic nature of health—individuals who will help tailor dietary changes that are practical, sustainable, and sensitive to your unique health needs and tastes.

The fruition of a thoughtfully crafted diet is not only evidenced by physical well-being but also mental and emotional health improvements. As we nourish our bodies adequately, our capacity to handle stress, engage fully in activities, and enjoy a sense of vitality, can flourish remarkably. In this age of information overload, where contradictory advice abounds, grounding our dietary choices in sound, holistic principles and personal attunement can lead to profoundly transformative health outcomes. Remember, the journey to health through better nutrition is a continuous one; every step—no matter how small—counts towards a healthier tomorrow.

LISTENING TO YOUR BODY

In the chorus of everyday life, our bodies often sing a subtle tune—a frequency that speaks in whispers, signaling our physical and emotional states. The art of listening to one's body is akin to learning a new language, one that communicates through sensations, reactions, and instinctual cues. Understanding this language requires attention, practice, and patience, as it unveils deeper insights into our health and what our systems truly require to thrive.

The journey of tuning into our bodies often begins with the recognition that each feeling or symptom—be it fatigue, irritability, or a craving—has an underlying message. These messages are our bodies' ways of guiding us towards equilibrium. To illustrate, consider the simple act of dehydration. Your body might signal its need for water through a dry mouth, headache, or dizziness. Rather than just addressing these symptoms in isolation, understanding and responding to them holistically can restore balance and wellbeing.

The Signals Speak: Deciphering What Your Body Needs

Our bodies communicate needs in various forms, often through what we might initially perceive as discomfort or pain. For instance, a series of digestive disturbances after meals may be your body's way of saying it struggles with certain types or amounts of food. Similarly, persistent skin issues like eczema or acne could be indicative of dietary intolerances or imbalances, environmental allergens, or stress-related hormonal changes.

Learning to interpret these signs effectively is a skill that embodies the principle of preventive health care. For example, regular occurrences of heartburn or acid reflux might lead one to consider not just the immediate relief provided by antacids but also deeper dietary adjustments and stress management techniques.

Emotional Appetites and Physical Health

Our emotional health is profoundly interconnected with our physical health, often communicating its state through physical sensations. Emotional stress, if chronic, can manifest physically in numerous ways—through constant fatigue, a compromised immune response, or even gastrointestinal issues. Recognizing these patterns can prompt us to integrate practices like meditation, adequate sleep, nutrition, and physical activity into our routine, aiming for a balanced lifestyle that honors both our emotional and physical needs. An intriguing aspect of listening to our body is understanding our cravings and differentiating them between psychological cravings and nutritional needs. Often, a craving for chocolate is not just a call for sugar but perhaps for magnesium, which is abundant in cocoa. Similarly, craving crunchy, salty snacks might reflect stress or frustration, where the act of crunching provides a pseudo-release of tension.

Intuitive Eating: The Dialogue of Nourishment

Intuitive eating emerges as a profound practice in the realm of listening to one's body. This approach invites us to eat based on physiological hunger signals rather than emotional triggers or strict dietary regimes. It fosters a compassionate, understanding relationship with food and body image, which stands in poignant contrast to restrictive dieting which often leads to cycles of binge eating and guilt.

This method encourages a diet that aligns closely with the body's natural hunger, fullness, and satiety cues, promoting a satisfying and nourishing relationship with food. By cultivating an awareness of these cues, we equip ourselves with the tools to make choices that respect our body's needs, enhancing our overall wellbeing.

The Role of Rest and Recharge

Our bodies also communicate the need for rest—something as essential as nutrition but often neglected in our productivity-driven society. Overlooking the signals for rest can lead to burnout and a decline in both mental and physical health. Listening to your body when it demands rest, whether it's through taking short breaks during a busy day or ensuring ample sleep each night, is crucial for maintaining overall health and vitality.

Implementing a Practice of Listening

Starting a daily practice of checking in with your body can cultivate this attentive listening. This might involve pausing at various times during the day to assess what you are feeling physically and emotionally, or it could be a more structured practice such as keeping a journal to record any symptoms or feelings, and noting what foods or activities precede them.

Embrace this process as a journey rather than a destination; there will be days when the signals might seem confounding or when old habits overshadow mindful listening. However, over time, this practice can enhance your ability to make informed, health-supporting decisions that are in tune with your body's natural rhythms and needs. In conclusion, the art of listening to one's body is akin to developing a deeply personal dialogue with oneself.

It's about building a relationship based on respect, attentiveness, and care that supports lifelong health and wellbeing. Through understanding and responding to our bodies' signals, we not only address the root causes of discomfort but also foster a state of health that radiates from the inside out.

Special Dietary Considerations

As diverse as humanity itself, dietary needs vary massively from one individual to another. These needs can be molded by a variety most conditions, such as allergies, sensitivities, metabolic rates, chronic conditions, and even more transient states like pregnancy. Truly, what works as nourishment for one might be a poison to another, making personalized nutrition not just preferable but essential.

The Body's Unique Language of Needs

Each body speaks its language of what it needs and what harms it. Consider celiac disease—an autoimmune disorder where the ingestion of gluten leads to damage in the small intestine. For individuals with this condition, a gluten-free diet is not a lifestyle choice but a necessity. Here, the body clearly signals that gluten is a harmful invader, triggering an immune response that is damaging.

Similarly, lactose intolerance is another prevalent issue where the body lacks the enzyme lactase, necessary to break down lactose, the sugar found in milk and other dairy products. Consumption of these products by lactose intolerant individuals can lead to discomfort at best and severe digestive distress at worst.

The Interplay Between Diet and Chronic Illness

Dietary considerations take on heightened importance in the presence of chronic conditions such as diabetes, heart disease, and various autoimmune disorders. For instance, individuals with diabetes must navigate their diets with an eye towards managing blood sugar levels. This involves not only monitoring the intake of sugars and carbohydrates but also understanding how various foods can either stabilize or destabilize glucose levels.

Heart disease patients, on the other hand, need to manage factors like cholesterol and blood pressure, which can be heavily influenced by diet. High sodium intake, for example, is linked to elevated blood pressure, while saturated and trans fats can lead to worse cholesterol levels, hence a diet low in these components becomes crucial.

Listening to the Less Heard: Food Sensitivities and Allergens

Apart from well-known conditions, there are subtler, yet significant, dietary sensitivities and allergies that might be less pronounced but equally impactful on one's health. Often, these sensitivities manifest as vague symptoms that can be challenging to trace back to specific dietary causes without careful observation and sometimes, medical testing. For example, someone might experience regular headaches, digestive distress, or even mood fluctuations, not realizing these could be reactions to certain foods. Identifying such links requires a combination of vigilance, dietary modification, and professional consultation.

Aligning Diet With Genetic Make-Up

Recent advancements in nutrigenomics—the study of how our genes interact with our nutrition—provide profound insights into how individual genetic makeup can dictate nutritional needs. Some individuals might metabolize caffeine quickly, experiencing little to no sleep disruption, whereas others with different genetic variants may be awake all night with the same amount of coffee.

Ethical and Environmental Considerations

Beyond health, personal ethics and environmental concerns are increasingly prominent in dietary considerations. Vegetarianism, veganism, and plant-based diets not only reflect personal ethical beliefs regarding animal rights and welfare but are also chosen for their reduced environmental impact relative to diets high in meat and animal products.

Crafting a Compassionate Path to Dietary Awareness

Embracing dietary diversity requires an open, informed, and compassionate approach. It involves not only learning about various dietary needs and conditions but also creating an inclusive environment where these can be accommodatively discussed and catered to. Integrating this understanding in family kitchens, community centers, and restaurants can contribute significantly to public health and harmony.

The first step towards embracing this broad spectrum of dietary needs is through education and awareness. Familiarize yourself with the common—and not so common—dietary restrictions and consider them when planning meals, not just for yourself but for social gatherings. Encouraging conversations about dietary needs without stigma or discomfort can help everyone dine with ease and enjoyment.

ENHANCING DIGESTIVE HEALTH

Imagine the journey of food: starting in the mouth, moving down the esophagus, being broken down in the stomach, absorbed in the intestines, and finally, the waste being expelled. Along this complex pathway, myriad issues can arise, often manifesting as symptoms such as bloating, gas, constipation, or irritable bowel syndrome (IBS). These are not merely discomforts but signals, much like the warning lights on a car's dashboard indicating that something needs attention.

The Foundation of Good Digestion: Balance and Awareness

The cornerstone of enhancing digestive health begins with balance — balancing the types of food we eat, the timing of meals, and our emotional states while consuming those meals. Stress, as often overlooked, plays a significant factor in digestive health. During stress, digestion is notably slowed or sometimes paused — a throwback to ancient survival mechanisms. This in mind, cultivating a practice of mindful eating where one not only pays attention to what is eaten but also how, when, and in what emotional state, can significantly soothe digestive turmoil.

Fiber: The Unsung Hero of Digestive Health

Fiber plays a crucial role in not just promoting satiety but also in smoothing the passage of food through the digestive tract. Think of fiber like a broom, sweeping through the intestines, aiding in bulk formation, and ensuring regular elimination. A diet rich in both soluble and insoluble fiber from a variety of sources such as fruits, vegetables, whole grains, and legumes is essential for healthy digestion.

Hydration: Easing Digestive Flow

Water is an often underestimated hero when it comes to digestion. It works synergistically with fiber, helping to soften stool and prevent constipation. Moreover, adequate hydration is crucial for saliva production and the proper functioning of gastric juices, which aid in breaking down food more effectively.

The Microbiome: A Complex Ecosystem Within

A flourishing community of microorganisms resides within our gut, playing myriad roles from aiding digestion to influencing mood and immune function. The composition of this microbiome is sensitive to diet, lifestyle, and even medications like antibiotics, which can disrupt its balance. Incorporating probiotic-rich foods such as yogurt, kefir, sauerkraut, and other fermented foods, or prebiotics found in foods like garlic, onions, and bananas, can help nourish and rebuild this vital community.

Listening to Your Body: Recognizing and Responding to Digestive Cues

Understanding and responding to the body's cues is paramount. Chronic indigestion, heartburn, or irregular bowel movements are not just nuisances but perhaps signs of underlying issues that need addressing — whether it be dietary adjustments, stress management techniques, or consulting with a healthcare provider.

Incorporating Herbal Allies

Certain herbs like peppermint, ginger, and chamomile have been celebrated through ages for their digestive benefits. Peppermint, for instance, has been shown to help relieve symptoms of IBS, while ginger can help reduce nausea and support digestion.

The Role of Physical Movement

Simple physical activities, such as walking or gentle yoga, can greatly enhance digestion by stimulating intestinal activity and helping to manage stress.

Setting the Stage: Environment Matters

The environment in which we eat our food can be just as important as the food itself. Eating in a calm, serene environment, seated comfortably, without the distraction of electronic devices, can help facilitate the digestive processes, allowing the body to focus fully on the task at hand - digestion.

2. BREAKFAST

OMEGA POWER SMOOTHIE BOWL

PREPARATION TIME: 10 min

COOKING TIME: 0 min

MODE OF COOKING: Blending

SERVINGS: 2

INGREDIENTS:

- 1 ripe banana, sliced and frozen
- 1/2 cup blueberries, frozen
- 1/4 cup raspberries, frozen
- 2 Tbsp chia seeds
- 1 Tbsp flaxseed meal
- 2 cups spinach, fresh
- 1 scoop protein powder (preferably plant-based)
- 1 cup unsweetened almond milk
- 1 Tbsp almond butter
- Toppings: sliced almonds, shredded coconut, additional berries

DIRECTIONS:

1. In a high-powered blender, combine the banana, blueberries, raspberries, chia seeds, flaxseed meal, spinach, protein powder, almond milk, and almond butter.
2. Blend on high until smooth and creamy. You may need to pause and stir or tamp down the mix a few times to ensure everything blends evenly.
3. Pour the smoothie mixture into bowls.
4. Garnish with sliced almonds, shredded coconut, and additional berries as desired.

TIPS:

- Ensure fruits are fully frozen to give the bowl a thick, ice-cream-like consistency.
- Experiment with different toppings like granola, pumpkin seeds, or a drizzle of honey for extra flavor and crunch.

NUTRITIONAL VALUES: Calories: 320, Fat: 14g, Carbs: 36g, Protein: 12g, Sugar: 14g

ANTI-INFLAMMATORY TURMERIC OATMEAL

PREPARATION TIME: 5 min

COOKING TIME: 15 min

MODE OF COOKING: Simmering

SERVINGS: 2

INGREDIENTS:

- 1 cup rolled oats
- 2 cups water or almond milk
- 1/2 tsp ground turmeric

- 1/4 tsp ground cinnamon
- 1 Tbsp flaxseed meal
- 1 Tbsp honey or maple syrup
- 1 apple, diced
- 1/4 cup walnuts, chopped
- A pinch of salt

DIRECTIONS:

1. In a medium saucepan, bring the water or almond milk to a boil.
2. Add the rolled oats and a pinch of salt, then reduce the heat to a simmer.
3. Stir in the turmeric, cinnamon, and flaxseed meal.
4. Cook for about 10-15 minutes on low heat, stirring occasionally until the oats are soft and have absorbed most of the liquid.
5. Remove from heat and stir in the honey or maple syrup.
6. Serve into bowls, and top with diced apple and chopped walnuts.

TIPS:

- For a creamier texture, you can substitute part of the water with coconut milk.
- Add a scoop of protein powder for an extra protein boost.
- Top with a spoonful of Greek yogurt for added creaminess and probiotics.

NUTRITIONAL VALUES: Calories: 295, Fat: 8g, Carbs: 49g, Protein: 8g, Sugar: 15g

Turmeric Ginger Oatmeal

PREPARATION TIME: 10 min
COOKING TIME: 15 min
MODE OF COOKING: Simmering
SERVINGS: 2
INGREDIENTS:

- 1 cup rolled oats
- 2 cups water
- 1/2 tsp ground turmeric
- 1/2 tsp ground ginger
- 1/4 tsp cinnamon
- 1 Tbsp honey
- 1/4 cup almond milk
- 1 Tbsp chia seeds
- 1 apple, cored and chopped
- 2 Tbsp chopped almonds

DIRECTIONS:

1. In a medium saucepan, bring water to a boil.
2. Add the oats, turmeric, ginger, and cinnamon. Reduce heat to a low simmer and cook for about 10-12 min, stirring occasionally, until the oats are soft and have absorbed most of the water.

3. Remove from heat and stir in honey, almond milk, and chia seeds.
4. Serve hot, topped with chopped apple and almonds.

TIPS:
- Add a pinch of black pepper to enhance the absorption of turmeric.
- For a creamier texture, use a blend of water and milk instead of just water.
- Top with a dollop of Greek yogurt for extra protein.

NUTRITIONAL VALUES: Calories: 290, Fat: 9g, Carbs: 49g, Protein: 8g, Sugar: 15g

Quinoa & Blueberry Breakfast Porridge

PREPARATION TIME: 5 min
COOKING TIME: 15 min
MODE OF COOKING: Boiling
SERVINGS: 2

INGREDIENTS:
- 1 cup quinoa, rinsed
- 2 cups water
- 1/2 cup fresh blueberries
- 1/4 tsp cinnamon
- 1 Tbsp honey
- 1/2 cup almond milk
- 1/4 cup chopped walnuts

DIRECTIONS:
1. Combine quinoa and water in a medium saucepan and bring to a boil over high heat.
2. Reduce heat to low and simmer until the quinoa is fully cooked and water is absorbed, about 15 minutes.
3. Remove from heat and stir in almond milk, cinnamon, and honey.
4. Gently fold in fresh blueberries and top with chopped walnuts.

TIPS:
- For added sweetness, drizzle additional honey or maple syrup over the top before serving.
- Substitute blueberries with other seasonal berries for variety.
- Add a pinch of nutmeg for extra warmth and flavor.

NUTRITIONAL VALUES: Calories: 285, Fat: 9.2g, Carbs: 44g, Protein: 8g, Sugar: 12g

Quinoa & Spinach Breakfast Muffins

PREPARATION TIME: 20 min

COOKING TIME: 25 min

MODE OF COOKING: Baking

SERVINGS: 12 muffins

INGREDIENTS:

- 1 cup quinoa, rinsed
- 2 cups fresh spinach, finely chopped
- 1/2 cup red bell pepper, finely diced
- 1/4 cup green onions, sliced
- 1/2 cup feta cheese, crumbled
- 4 large eggs, beaten
- 1/2 tsp garlic powder
- Salt and pepper to taste
- 1/2 tsp paprika
- Olive oil spray for greasing

DIRECTIONS:

1. Preheat the oven to 375°F (190°C). Grease a 12-cup muffin tin with olive oil spray.
2. Cook quinoa according to the package instructions, then let it cool slightly.
3. In a large bowl, combine the cooled quinoa, chopped spinach, red bell pepper, green onions, and feta cheese.
4. In another bowl, whisk together the eggs, garlic powder, paprika, salt, and pepper.
5. Pour the egg mixture over the quinoa mixture and stir until well combined.
6. Spoon the mixture into the prepared muffin tin, filling each cup to the top.
7. Bake in the preheated oven for 25 minutes, or until the tops are golden brown and a toothpick inserted into the center comes out clean.
8. Allow to cool for 5 minutes before removing from the tin.

TIPS:

- These muffins can be stored in an airtight container in the refrigerator for up to 5 days.
- Serve warm or at room temperature for a quick and nutritious breakfast option.
- For a non-dairy version, substitute the feta cheese with nutritional yeast to maintain a cheesy flavor.

NUTRITIONAL VALUES: Calories: 150, Fat: 6g, Carbs: 18g, Protein: 8g, Sugar: 1g

Ginger Pear Oatmeal

PREPARATION TIME: 5 min

COOKING TIME: 15 min

MODE OF COOKING: Simmering

SERVINGS: 2

INGREDIENTS:
- 1 cup rolled oats
- 2 cups water or almond milk
- 1 pear, peeled and diced
- 1 Tbsp freshly grated ginger
- 1 tsp cinnamon
- 2 Tbsp honey or maple syrup
- Pinch of salt

DIRECTIONS:
1. In a medium saucepan, bring the water or almond milk to a boil.
2. Add the oats and a pinch of salt to the boiling liquid, reduce the heat to low, and simmer for 10 minutes, stirring occasionally.
3. Add the diced pear, grated ginger, and cinnamon to the oatmeal.
4. Continue to simmer for another 5 minutes, or until the oatmeal is creamy and the pears are tender.
5. Stir in honey or maple syrup to sweeten, and serve warm.

TIPS:
- Top with a sprinkle of chopped nuts for added texture and protein.
- Add a dollop of yogurt for creaminess and a boost of probiotics.

NUTRITIONAL VALUES: Calories: 235, Fat: 2g, Carbs: 49g, Protein: 6g, Sugar: 20g

Quinoa & Spinach Power Breakfast

PREPARATION TIME: 10 min

COOKING TIME: 20 min

MODE OF COOKING: Boiling

SERVINGS: 4

INGREDIENTS:
- 1 cup quinoa, rinsed
- 2 cups water
- 1 Tbsp coconut oil
- 2 cups fresh spinach, chopped
- 4 eggs
- 1/2 tsp salt
- 1/4 tsp black pepper
- 1/4 cup feta cheese, crumbled
- 1/4 cup fresh parsley, chopped
- 1 avocado, peeled and sliced

DIRECTIONS:

1. In a medium saucepan, bring the quinoa and water to a boil. Reduce heat to low, cover, and simmer until the quinoa is tender and the water is absorbed, about 15 min.
2. Heat the coconut oil in a skillet over medium heat. Add the chopped spinach and sauté until wilted, about 3-4 min.
3. Stir the cooked spinach into the cooked quinoa.
4. In the same skillet, crack the eggs and fry them to your liking, seasoning with salt and pepper.
5. Divide the quinoa and spinach mixture among four plates.
6. Place one fried egg on top of each serving of quinoa and spinach.
7. Sprinkle crumbled feta cheese and chopped parsley over each dish.
8. Add slices of avocado to each plate before serving.

TIPS:

- For a vegan option, omit the eggs and feta cheese, and top with a dollop of hummus or a sprinkle of nutritional yeast.
- Add a dash of hot sauce or a sprinkle of chili flakes for an extra kick.
- Cooking quinoa in vegetable or chicken broth instead of water can add more flavor to the dish.

NUTRITIONAL VALUES: Calories: 320, Fat: 15g, Carbs: 35g, Protein: 13g, Sugar: 2g

QUINOA & SPINACH POWER BREAKFAST BOWL

PREPARATION TIME: 10 min
COOKING TIME: 20 min
MODE OF COOKING: Boiling
SERVINGS: 2
INGREDIENTS:

- 1 cup quinoa, rinsed
- 2 cups water
- 1/2 teaspoon salt
- 2 cups fresh spinach, chopped
- 4 eggs
- 1 avocado, sliced
- 1/2 teaspoon freshly ground black pepper
- 4 Tbsp salsa (optional)

DIRECTIONS:

1. In a saucepan, bring water to a boil. Add quinoa and salt, reduce heat to low, cover, and simmer for 15 minutes or until all water is absorbed.
2. Add the chopped spinach to the

cooked quinoa, cover the pan, and let sit for 3 minutes for the spinach to wilt. Fluff with a fork to mix in the spinach.

3. Meanwhile, in another saucepan, bring water to a gentle boil. Carefully add the eggs and cook for about 7 minutes for a softer yolk or 10 minutes for hard-boiled. Remove from heat, drain, and cool under cold running water before peeling.

4. Divide the quinoa and spinach mixture between two bowls. Top each with two peeled eggs, sliced avocado, and a sprinkle of black pepper.

5. Serve each bowl with 2 tablespoons of salsa if desired.

TIPS:

- For added flavor, cook the quinoa in vegetable or chicken broth instead of water.
- Add a drizzle of olive oil or a squeeze of lemon juice on top for an extra layer of taste.
- Replace spinach with kale or Swiss chard for a variation in greens.

NUTRITIONAL VALUES: Calories: 420, Fat: 19g, Carbs: 42g, Protein: 20g, Sugar: 2g

---

SPICED QUINOA & CHIA BREAKFAST BOWL

PREPARATION TIME: 15 min
COOKING TIME: 20 min
MODE OF COOKING: Simmering
SERVINGS: 4
INGREDIENTS:

- 1 cup quinoa, rinsed and drained
- 2 cups water
- 4 Tbsp chia seeds
- 1 tsp cinnamon
- 1/2 tsp nutmeg
- 2 Tbsp honey or maple syrup
- 1/2 cup fresh blueberries
- 1/2 cup sliced strawberries
- 1/4 cup crushed walnuts
- 1/4 cup almond slices
- Almond milk, for serving

DIRECTIONS:

1. In a medium saucepan, combine quinoa and water. Bring to a boil over high heat.
2. Reduce heat to low, cover, and simmer for 15 minutes or until the quinoa is cooked and water is absorbed.
3. Remove from heat and stir in chia seeds, cinnamon, and nutmeg.
4. Cover and let sit for 5 minutes,

allowing the chia seeds to swell and absorb moisture.
5. Stir in honey or maple syrup, mixing thoroughly.
6. Serve in bowls, topped with fresh blueberries, strawberries, crushed walnuts, and almond slices.
7. Add a splash of almond milk to each bowl for added creaminess.

TIPS:
- Customize your bowl with seasonal fruits for variety and added nutrition.
- For a vegan option, ensure that maple syrup is used instead of honey.
- Add a scoop of protein powder for an extra protein boost in your meal.

NUTRITIONAL VALUES: Calories: 275, Fat: 9g, Carbs: 39g, Protein: 8g, Sugar: 10g

3. SOUPS

HEALING GINGER-TURMERIC CARROT SOUP

PREPARATION TIME: 15 min
COOKING TIME: 30 min
MODE OF COOKING: Simmering
SERVINGS: 4
INGREDIENTS:

- 1 Tbsp coconut oil
- 1 medium onion, chopped
- 3 cloves garlic, minced
- 2 Tbsp fresh ginger, grated
- 1 Tbsp fresh turmeric, grated (or 1 tsp dried turmeric)
- 1 lb carrots, peeled and diced
- 4 cups vegetable broth
- 1 can (14 oz) coconut milk
- Salt and pepper to taste
- Fresh cilantro, for garnish

DIRECTIONS:

1. Heat the coconut oil in a large pot over medium heat. Add the onion and sauté until translucent, about 5 min.
2. Add the garlic, ginger, and turmeric, stirring continuously for about 1 min to release the flavors.
3. Mix in the diced carrots, then pour in the vegetable broth. Bring the mixture to a boil.
4. Reduce the heat and let it simmer, covered, for 20 min or until the carrots are tender.
5. Remove from heat and blend the soup using an immersion blender until smooth.
6. Stir in the coconut milk and season with salt and pepper. Heat through.
7. Serve hot, garnished with fresh cilantro.

TIPS:

- For a spicier kick, add a pinch of cayenne pepper with the turmeric.
- If using dried turmeric, ensure it is fresh for the best flavor and health benefits.
- Serve with a crusty whole-grain bread for a wholesome meal.

NUTRITIONAL VALUES: Calories: 215, Fat: 14g, Carbs: 22g, Protein: 3g, Sugar: 10g

Ginger-Spiced Pumpkin Soup

PREPARATION TIME: 20 min

COOKING TIME: 45 min

MODE OF COOKING: Simmering

SERVINGS: 6

INGREDIENTS:

- 1 Tbsp olive oil
- 1 large onion, finely chopped
- 2 garlic cloves, minced
- 2 tsp ground ginger
- 1 tsp ground cinnamon
- 1/4 tsp ground nutmeg
- 1 large pumpkin (about 3 lb), peeled, seeded, and cubed
- 4 cups vegetable broth
- 1 cup coconut milk
- Salt and pepper to taste
- Pumpkin seeds (for garnish)

PROCEDURE:

1. Heat the olive oil in a large pot over medium heat. Add the chopped onion and garlic, sautéing until the onion becomes translucent, about 5 min.
2. Stir in the ground ginger, cinnamon, and nutmeg, cooking for another 2 min. until the spices are fragrant.
3. Add the cubed pumpkin to the pot, tossing to coat it well with the spices.
4. Pour in the vegetable broth, increase the heat to high and bring to a boil. Once boiling, reduce the heat to low, cover, and let it simmer for 30 min. or until the pumpkin is tender.
5. Use an immersion blender to puree the soup directly in the pot until smooth. Alternatively, carefully transfer the soup in batches to a blender to puree.
6. Stir in the coconut milk, and continue to heat the soup for another 5 min. Season with salt and pepper to taste.
7. Serve hot, garnished with pumpkin seeds.

TIPS:

- For a creamier texture, add an extra 1/2 cup of coconut milk.
- Garnish with a swirl of cream or a sprinkle of cinnamon for enhanced flavor.
- Roasting the pumpkin prior to adding it to the soup can intensify the flavor.

NUTRITIONAL VALUES:

Calories: 180; Fat: 9g; Carbs: 24g; Protein: 4g; Sugar: 6g

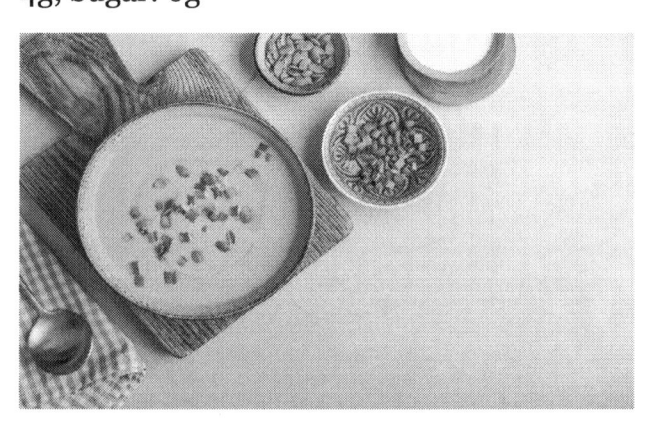

Healing Turmeric Ginger Soup

PREPARATION TIME: 20 min
COOKING TIME: 35 min
MODE OF COOKING: Simmering
SERVINGS: 4
INGREDIENTS:

- 1 Tbsp olive oil
- 1 medium onion, finely chopped
- 2 cloves garlic, minced
- 2 Tbsp fresh ginger, grated
- 1 Tbsp turmeric powder
- 1 carrot, diced
- 1 stalk celery, diced
- 4 cups vegetable broth
- 1 cup coconut milk
- 1 cup kale, chopped
- Juice of 1 lemon
- Salt and pepper to taste

DIRECTIONS:

1. In a large pot, heat the olive oil over medium heat. Add onions and garlic, sauté until the onions become translucent.
2. Stir in the ginger and turmeric, cook for another 2 min until fragrant.
3. Add the diced carrots and celery to the pot, cook for 5 min, stirring occasionally.
4. Pour in the vegetable broth and bring the mixture to a boil. Reduce heat and simmer for 20 min.
5. Stir in the coconut milk and chopped kale, continue cooking for another 5 min.
6. Remove from heat and stir in fresh lemon juice. Season with salt and pepper to taste.

TIPS:

- Enhance the soup's healing properties by adding a pinch of black pepper, which increases the absorption of turmeric.
- For a heartier meal, you can add shredded chicken or soft tofu.
- Serve hot, garnished with a sprig of fresh cilantro for added flavor.

NUTRITIONAL VALUES: Calories: 150, Fat: 9g, Carbs: 13g, Protein: 3g, Sugar: 5g

Gingered Butternut Squash Soup

PREPARATION TIME: 20 min
COOKING TIME: 45 min
MODE OF COOKING: Simmering
SERVINGS: 6
INGREDIENTS:

- 1 medium butternut squash, peeled

- and cubed (about 6 cups)
- 1 Tbsp extra virgin olive oil
- 1 medium onion, diced
- 3 cloves garlic, minced
- 2 Tbsp fresh ginger, minced
- 4 cups vegetable broth
- 1 cup coconut milk
- 1 tsp sea salt
- 1/2 tsp black pepper
- 1/4 tsp nutmeg
- Fresh cilantro for garnish

PROCEDURE:

1. Heat the olive oil in a large pot over medium heat. Add the diced onion and sauté until translucent, about 5 min.
2. Add minced garlic and ginger, sautéing for another 2 min until fragrant.
3. Stir in the cubed butternut squash, tossing to coat with the onion, garlic, and ginger mixture.
4. Pour in the vegetable broth and bring the mixture to a boil. Once boiling, reduce the heat and let it simmer, covered, for about 30 min or until the squash is tender.
5. Carefully blend the soup using an immersion blender until smooth and creamy.
6. Stir in the coconut milk, and season with salt, pepper, and nutmeg. Heat for an additional 5 min.
7. Serve warm, garnished with fresh cilantro.

TIPS:

- For a deeper flavor, roast the butternut squash at 400°F (204°C) for 25 min before adding it to the soup.
- Top with a dollop of Greek yogurt or sour cream if desired for extra creaminess.
- For a vegan option, use coconut yogurt or omit the yogurt topping entirely.

NUTRITIONAL VALUES: Calories: 183, Fat: 9g, Carbs: 26g, Protein: 3g, Sugar: 6g

---

HEALING GINGER CARROT SOUP

PREPARATION TIME: 20 min
COOKING TIME: 30 min
MODE OF COOKING: Simmering
SERVINGS: 4

INGREDIENTS:

- 1 Tbsp olive oil
- 1 onion, finely chopped
- 3 cloves garlic, minced
- 2 Tbsp fresh ginger, grated

- 1 pound carrots, peeled and diced
- 4 cups vegetable broth
- 1 tsp turmeric powder
- Salt and pepper to taste
- 1 can (14 oz.) coconut milk
- Fresh cilantro, for garnish

DIRECTIONS:

1. Heat olive oil in a large pot over medium heat. Add chopped onion and garlic, sauté until onion becomes translucent.
2. Stir in grated ginger and diced carrots, sauté for another 5 minutes until the carrots begin to soften.
3. Pour in vegetable broth, add turmeric powder, salt, and pepper. Bring to a boil, then reduce heat and let simmer for 20 minutes, or until carrots are completely soft.
4. Use an immersion blender to puree the soup directly in the pot until smooth.
5. Stir in coconut milk and heat through for another 5 minutes. Adjust seasoning as needed.
6. Serve hot, garnished with fresh cilantro.

TIPS:

- Add a squeeze of fresh lime juice just before serving to enhance the flavors.
- For a touch of sweetness, add a small apple, peeled and diced, with the carrots.
- If a thicker consistency is desired, reduce the amount of vegetable broth slightly.

NUTRITIONAL VALUES: Calories: 235, Fat: 15g, Carbs: 22g, Protein: 3g, Sugar: 7g

HEALING GINGER-PUMPKIN SOUP

PREPARATION TIME: 20 min
COOKING TIME: 45 min
MODE OF COOKING: Simmering
SERVINGS: 6
INGREDIENTS:

- 2 Tbsp olive oil
- 1 medium onion, chopped
- 4 cups pumpkin, peeled and cubed
- 3 Tbsp freshly grated ginger
- 4 cups vegetable broth
- 1 can (14 oz) coconut milk
- 1 tsp ground cinnamon
- Salt and pepper to taste
- Pumpkin seeds for garnish (optional)

DIRECTIONS:

1. Heat the olive oil in a large pot over medium heat. Add the chopped onions and sauté until they are translucent,

about 5 minutes.
2. Add the pumpkin cubes and grated ginger to the pot, stirring for another 5 minutes.
3. Pour in the vegetable broth and bring the mixture to a boil. Once boiling, reduce the heat and let it simmer until the pumpkin is tender, about 30 minutes.
4. Use an immersion blender to purée the soup directly in the pot until smooth. Alternatively, you can transfer the mixture to a blender and blend in batches.
5. Stir in the coconut milk, ground cinnamon, and season with salt and pepper. Warm the soup for an additional 5 min.
6. Serve hot and if desired, garnish with pumpkin seeds for added crunch.

TIPS:
- For an extra kick, add a pinch of cayenne pepper.
- If fresh pumpkin is not available, canned pure pumpkin can also work well in this recipe.
- To enhance the flavors, roast the pumpkin cubes before adding them to the soup.

NUTRITIONAL VALUES: Calories: 215, Fat: 14g, Carbs: 23g, Protein: 3g, Sugar: 9g.

Soothing Ginger Turmeric Soup

PREPARATION TIME: 10 min
COOKING TIME: 20 min
MODE OF COOKING: Simmering
SERVINGS: 4
INGREDIENTS:
- 1 Tbsp olive oil
- 1 medium onion, diced
- 2 cloves garlic, minced
- 2 Tbsp fresh ginger, peeled and minced
- 1 Tbsp turmeric powder
- 4 cups vegetable broth
- 1 carrot, peeled and diced
- 1 stalk celery, diced
- 1 cup chopped kale
- Salt and pepper, to taste
- 1 Tbsp lemon juice
- Fresh cilantro, chopped for garnish

DIRECTIONS:
1. Heat olive oil in a large pot over medium heat.
2. Add onion and garlic, sauté until onions are translucent, about 2-3 min.
3. Stir in ginger and turmeric, cook for

another minute until fragrant.
4. Pour in vegetable broth and bring the mixture to a boil.
5. Reduce heat to low, add carrots, and celery, simmer for 10 min.
6. Add chopped kale, continue to simmer for an additional 5 min or until all vegetables are tender.
7. Season with salt and pepper, and stir in lemon juice.
8. Serve hot, garnished with fresh cilantro.

TIPS:
- Adding a pinch of black pepper can increase the absorption of turmeric.
- For added protein, consider adding a can of rinsed and drained chickpeas.
- If you prefer a creamy soup, blend half the soup with an immersion blender before serving.

NUTRITIONAL VALUES: Calories: 90, Fat: 3.5g, Carbs: 13g, Protein: 2g, Sugar: 4g

HEALING TURMERIC LENTIL SOUP

PREPARATION TIME: 15 min
COOKING TIME: 30 min
MODE OF COOKING: Simmering
SERVINGS: 6
INGREDIENTS:
- 1 cup dried red lentils, rinsed
- 2 Tbsp olive oil
- 1 onion, finely chopped
- 3 garlic cloves, minced
- 2 carrots, diced
- 2 tsp ground turmeric
- 1 tsp ground cumin
- 1/2 tsp ground cinnamon
- 1 quart vegetable broth
- 1 can (14 oz.) diced tomatoes
- Salt and freshly ground black pepper, to taste
- 3 cups chopped spinach
- 1 lemon, juiced
- Fresh cilantro, for garnish

DIRECTIONS:
1. In a large pot, heat the olive oil over medium heat. Add the chopped onion and minced garlic, sautéing until the onion becomes translucent, about 5 min.
2. Stir in the diced carrots and cook for 3 more min, ensuring they get slightly soft.
3. Add the ground turmeric, cumin, and cinnamon, and stir well to coat the vegetables in the spices, allowing them

to become fragrant.

4. Pour in the vegetable broth and add the rinsed lentils along with the diced tomatoes. Bring the mixture to a boil, then reduce heat and let it simmer, covered, for about 20 min or until the lentils are tender.
5. Season with salt and pepper. Just before turning off the heat, add the chopped spinach and allow it to wilt in the soup.
6. Stir in the fresh lemon juice and adjust any seasoning as needed.
7. Serve hot, garnished with chopped fresh cilantro.

TIPS:
- The lemon juice added at the end helps to brighten the flavors; don't skip it!
- For a richer flavor, a dollop of coconut yogurt can be added when serving.
- This soup stores well and the flavors deepen when reheated, making it perfect for meal prep.

NUTRITIONAL VALUES: Calories: 215, Fat: 5g, Carbs: 33g, Protein: 10g, Sugar: 5g

HEALING GINGER PUMPKIN SOUP

PREPARATION TIME: 20 min
COOKING TIME: 45 min
MODE OF COOKING: Simmering
SERVINGS: 6
INGREDIENTS:
- 1 Tbsp olive oil
- 1 medium onion, chopped
- 3 cloves garlic, minced
- 2 Tbsp fresh ginger, grated
- 1 tsp turmeric powder
- 1/4 tsp cay cayenne pepper (optional)
- 4 cups pumpkin puree (fresh or canned)
- 4 cups vegetable broth
- 1 can (14 oz) coconut milk
- Salt and black pepper to taste
- Pumpkin seeds (for garnish)
- Fresh cilantro, chopped (for garnish)

PROCEDURE:
1. Heat the olive oil in a large pot over medium heat. Add the chopped onion and sauté until translucent, about 5 min.
2. Add the minced garlic, grated ginger, turmeric powder, and cayenne pepper. Cook for another 2 min, stirring frequently.
3. Pour in the pumpkin puree and vegetable broth. Stir well to combine all ingredients.

4. Bring the mixture to a boil, then reduce heat and let it simmer for 30 min, stirring occasionally.
5. Blend the soup using an immersion blender until smooth.
6. Stir in the coconut milk and continue to simmer for another 10 min. Season with salt and black pepper to taste.
7. Serve hot, garnished with pumpkin seeds and chopped fresh cilantro.

TIPS:
- If using fresh pumpkin, roast it first for a deeper flavor.
- Add a squeeze of fresh lime juice for an extra zing before serving.
- Serve with a side of toasted whole grain bread for a hearty meal.

NUTRITIONAL VALUES: Calories: 240, Fat: 13g, Carbs: 29g, Protein: 5g, Sugar: 12g

4. MAIN DISH

QUINOA & BLACK BEAN STUFFED PEPPERS

PREPARATION TIME: 20 min

COOKING TIME: 35 min

MODE OF COOKING: Baking

SERVINGS: 4

INGREDIENTS:

- 4 large bell peppers, tops cut off and seeds removed
- 1 cup quinoa, rinsed
- 2 cups vegetable broth
- 1 Tbsp olive oil
- 1 medium onion, finely chopped
- 2 cloves garlic, minced
- 1 tsp ground cumin
- 1 tsp smoked paprika
- 1 (15 oz.) can black beans, drained and rinsed
- 1 cup corn kernels (fresh or frozen)
- 1/2 cup chopped fresh cilantro
- Juice of 1 lime
- Salt and pepper to taste
- 1/2 cup grated cheese (optional, for topping)

DIRECTIONS:

1. Preheat oven to 375°F (190°C).
2. In a medium saucepan, combine quinoa and vegetable broth, bring to a boil. Reduce heat to low, cover, and simmer for 15 minutes, or until liquid is absorbed.
3. Heat olive oil in a skillet over medium heat. Add onions and garlic; sauté until onions are translucent, about 5 minutes.
4. Stir in cumin and smoked paprika, cook for an additional minute.
5. Combine cooked quinoa, sautéed onion mixture, black beans, corn, cilantro, and lime juice in a large bowl. Season with salt and pepper.
6. Stuff the mixture into the hollowed-out peppers, and place them upright in a baking dish.
7. Top each pepper with grated cheese if using.
8. Cover with foil and bake for 25 minutes. Remove foil and bake for another 10 minutes, or until peppers are tender and cheese is bubbly and golden.

TIPS:

- For a vegan option, omit the cheese or use a plant-based cheese alternative.
- If you like it spicy, add a diced jalapeño to the onion and garlic sauté.

- These stuffed peppers can be made ahead. Just assemble them, refrigerate, and bake just before serving.

NUTRITIONAL VALUES: Calories: 295, Fat: 7g, Carbs: 48g, Protein: 12g, Sugar: 8g

ZESTY LEMON HERB CHICKEN

PREPARATION TIME: 20 min
COOKING TIME: 45 min
MODE OF COOKING: Baking
SERVINGS: 4
INGREDIENTS:

- 4 chicken breasts, boneless and skinless
- 2 lemons, one juiced and one sliced
- 3 Tbsp olive oil
- 3 cloves garlic, minced
- 2 Tbsp fresh rosemary, chopped
- 2 Tbsp fresh thyme, chopped
- Salt and pepper to taste

DIRECTIONS:

1. Preheat the oven to 375°F (190°C).
2. In a large bowl, combine lemon juice, olive oil, garlic, rosemary, thyme, salt, and pepper.
3. Add chicken breasts to the marinade and ensure they are well-coated. Let marinate for at least 15 minutes in the fridge.
4. Place the marinated chicken in a baking dish, and arrange sliced lemons over the top.
5. Bake in preheated oven for approximately 45 minutes, or until chicken is fully cooked and juices run clear.
6. Occasionally baste the chicken with the pan juices to keep it moist.

TIPS:

- Garnish with additional fresh herbs before serving for enhanced flavor and presentation.
- Serve with a side of steamed vegetables or a fresh salad for a balanced meal.

NUTRITIONAL VALUES: Calories: 310, Fat: 14g, Carbs: 8g, Protein: 36g, Sugar: 2g

QUINOA & ROASTED VEGETABLE BOWL

PREPARATION TIME: 20 min

COOKING TIME: 30 min

MODE OF COOKING: Roasting and Boiling

SERVINGS: 4

INGREDIENTS:

- 1 cup quinoa, rinsed
- 2 cups water
- 1 small zucchini, cubed
- 1 red bell pepper, chopped
- 1 yellow bell pepper, chopped
- 1 medium carrot, cubed
- 1 Tbsp olive oil
- 1 tsp garlic powder
- 1 tsp dried oregano
- Salt and pepper to taste
- 1/4 cup chopped fresh parsley
- Juice of 1 lemon

PROCEDURE:

1. Preheat oven to 400°F (204°C).
2. In a medium saucepan, bring 2 cups of water to a boil. Add the quinoa, reduce heat to low, cover, and simmer for about 15 min until all the water is absorbed.
3. While the quinoa is cooking, toss zucchini, red bell pepper, yellow bell pepper, and carrot with olive oil, garlic powder, oregano, salt, and pepper.
4. Spread the vegetables on a baking sheet in a single layer and roast in the preheated oven for 20 min until they are tender and begin to brown.
5. Remove vegetables from the oven and let cool slightly.
6. In a large bowl, combine cooked quinoa and roasted vegetables. Add chopped parsley and drizzle with lemon juice.
7. Toss everything together to mix well and adjust seasoning as needed.

TIPS:

- For a protein boost, add chickpeas or diced chicken breast to the roasting vegetables.
- Use any combination of vegetables you have on hand; this dish is highly versatile.
- Serve warm or at room temperature, making it perfect for leftovers or meal prep.

NUTRITIONAL VALUES: Calories: 295, Fat: 7g, Carbs: 49g, Protein: 8g, Sugar: 7g

Lemon Garlic Roasted Chicken with Root Vegetables

PREPARATION TIME: 20 min

COOKING TIME: 1 hr 10 min

MODE OF COOKING: Roasting

SERVINGS: 6

INGREDIENTS:

- 1 whole chicken (about 4 lb)
- 3 Tbsp olive oil
- 4 cloves garlic, minced
- 1 lemon, halved
- 1 tsp dried rosemary
- 1 tsp dried thyme
- Salt and pepper to taste
- 2 carrots, peeled and chopped into 1-inch pieces
- 2 parsnips, peeled and chopped into 1-inch pieces
- 1 sweet potato, peeled and cubed
- 1 red onion, peeled and quartered

PROCEDURE:

1. Preheat the oven to 400°F (204°C).
2. Rinse the chicken and pat dry with paper towels. Season the cavity with salt and pepper, and stuff with one half of the lemon.
3. In a small bowl, combine olive oil, garlic, juice from the other lemon half, rosemary, thyme, salt, and pepper.
4. Rub the chicken all over with the olive oil mixture.
5. Arrange the chopped carrots, parsnips, sweet potato, and onion in a roasting tin and place the seasoned chicken on top of the vegetables.
6. Roast in the preheated oven for 1 hr 10 min or until the chicken is golden brown and the vegetables are tender. The internal temperature of the chicken should reach 165°F (74°C).
7. Remove from the oven and let the chicken rest for 10 minutes before carving.

TIPS:

- Insert a meat thermometer into the thickest part of the thigh, not touching the bone, to accurately check doneness.
- You can squeeze the roasted lemon over the chicken and vegetables for extra zing after cooking.
- Let the chicken rest covered with foil before carving to keep it juicy.

NUTRITIONAL VALUES: Calories: 450, Fat: 24g, Carbs: 18g, Protein: 40g, Sugar: 5g

QUINOA STUFFED BELL PEPPERS

PREPARATION TIME: 20 min
COOKING TIME: 40 min
MODE OF COOKING: Baking
SERVINGS: 4

INGREDIENTS:

- 4 large bell peppers, tops cut, seeds removed
- 1 cup quinoa, rinsed
- 2 Tbsp olive oil
- 1 medium onion, finely chopped
- 2 cloves garlic, minced
- 1 zucchini, diced
- 1 carrot, diced
- 1 tsp dried oregano
- 1 tsp dried basil
- Salt and pepper to taste
- 1/2 cup tomato sauce
- 1/2 cup shredded mozzarella cheese (optional)
- Fresh parsley, chopped for garnish

PROCEDURE:

1. Preheat oven to 375°F (190°C).
2. Cook quinoa according to package instructions and set aside.
3. In a skillet, heat olive oil over medium heat. Add onion and garlic, and sauté until translucent.
4. Add zucchini and carrot to the skillet. Cook until vegetables are tender.
5. Stir in the cooked quinoa, oregano, basil, salt, and pepper. Mix well.
6. Spoon the quinoa mixture into each bell pepper cavity.
7. Place the stuffed peppers in a baking dish and pour tomato sauce over each.
8. Cover with aluminum foil and bake in the preheated oven for 30 minutes.
9. Remove foil, top each pepper with mozzarella if using, and bake for another 10 minutes or until cheese is melted and slightly golden.
10. Garnish with fresh parsley before serving.

TIPS:

- Choose bell peppers that are similar in size to ensure even cooking.
- If you prefer a vegan version, omit the cheese or use a vegan cheese alternative.
- Add a protein source like chickpeas or black beans to the stuffing for a heartier dish.

NUTRITIONAL VALUES: Calories: 295, Fat: 9g, Carbs: 45g, Protein: 12g, Sugar: 9g

Turmeric-Spiced Quinoa with Roasted Vegetables

PREPARATION TIME: 20 min

COOKING TIME: 30 min

MODE OF COOKING: Roasting and Simmering

SERVINGS: 4

INGREDIENTS:

- 1 cup quinoa, rinsed
- 2 cups water
- 1 tsp turmeric powder
- 1/2 tsp black pepper
- 1 tsp sea salt, divided
- 1 small sweet potato, cubed
- 1 red bell pepper, chopped
- 1 zucchini, chopped
- 1 yellow squash, chopped
- 2 Tbsp olive oil
- 1/2 tsp garlic powder
- 1/4 cup fresh parsley, chopped
- Juice of 1 lemon

DIRECTIONS:

1. Preheat oven to 400°F (204°C).
2. In a medium saucepan, combine quinoa, water, turmeric, black pepper, and 1/2 tsp of sea salt. Bring to a boil, then cover and simmer for 15-20 min until the quinoa is tender and water is absorbed.
3. While quinoa cooks, in a large bowl, toss sweet potato, red bell pepper, zucchini, and yellow squash with olive oil, garlic powder, and remaining 1/2 tsp of sea salt.
4. Spread the vegetables on a baking sheet and roast in the preheated oven for about 20-25 min until tender and slightly caramelized, stirring halfway through.
5. Once both quinoa and vegetables are cooked, mix them together in a large bowl.
6. Add chopped parsley and drizzle with fresh lemon juice before serving.

TIPS:

- Ensure vegetables are cut in uniform sizes for even roasting.
- Serve this dish with a side of grilled chicken or fish for added protein.
- Lemon juice not only adds freshness but also enhances the absorption of turmeric's beneficial properties.

NUTRITIONAL VALUES: Calories: 290, Fat: 10g, Carbs: 44g, Protein: 8g, Sugar: 7g

QUINOA AND ROASTED VEGETABLE BOWL

PREPARATION TIME: 20 min
COOKING TIME: 30 min
MODE OF COOKING: Roasting/Baking
SERVINGS: 4

INGREDIENTS:

- 1 cup quinoa
- 2 cups water
- 1 small butternut squash, peeled and cubed
- 1 red bell pepper, cut into 1-inch pieces
- 1 zucchini, sliced into half-moons
- 1 red onion, cut into wedges
- 2 Tbsp olive oil
- 1 tsp smoked paprika
- Salt and pepper to taste
- 2 Tbsp pumpkin seeds
- 1 handful fresh arugula
- 1 Tbsp balsamic vinegar

DIRECTIONS:

1. Preheat the oven to 425°F (220°C).
2. Rinse the quinoa thoroughly under cold water and drain.
3. In a medium saucepan, combine quinoa and water. Bring to a boil, then cover and reduce to a simmer. Cook for 15 min until the quinoa is fluffy and the water is absorbed.
4. In a large mixing bowl, toss butternut squash, red bell pepper, zucchini, and red onion with olive oil, smoked paprika, salt, and pepper.
5. Spread the vegetables on a baking sheet and roast for 20-25 min until tender and slightly caramelized.
6. In a serving bowl, combine cooked quinoa and roasted vegetables. Top with pumpkin seeds and fresh arugula.
7. Drizzle balsamic vinegar over the bowl just before serving.

TIPS:

- For added protein, mix in chickpeas or diced grilled chicken.
- Spice up the dish with a sprinkle of chili flakes or a drizzle of sriracha sauce.
- Substitute any seasonal vegetables you prefer or have on hand.

NUTRITIONAL VALUES: Calories: 320, Fat: 10g, Carbs: 50g, Protein: 8g, Sugar: 5g

5. SNACK RECIPES

SPICED CHICKPEA CRUNCH

PREPARATION TIME: 10 min
COOKING TIME: 30 min
MODE OF COOKING: Baking
SERVINGS: 4

INGREDIENTS:

- 1 can (15 oz.) chickpeas, drained and rinsed
- 1 Tbsp olive oil
- 1 tsp smoked paprika
- 1 tsp garlic powder
- 1/2 tsp cumin
- 1/4 tsp cayenne pepper (optional for added heat)
- Salt to taste

DIRECTIONS:

1. Preheat your oven to 375°F (190°C).
2. Pat the chickpeas dry with paper towels, removing as much moisture as possible.
3. In a bowl, toss the chickpeas with olive oil, smoked paprika, garlic powder, cumin, cayenne pepper, and salt.
4. Spread the chickpeas in an even layer on a baking sheet lined with parchment paper.
5. Bake in the preheated oven for about 30 minutes, stirring every 10 minutes, until the chickpeas are golden and crispy.
6. Remove from the oven and let cool slightly before serving. They will continue to crisp up as they cool.

TIPS:

- For an extra flavor boost, squeeze a little lemon juice over the chickpeas before serving.
- Store any leftovers in an airtight container to maintain crispiness.
- Experiment with different spices like turmeric or za'atar for a variety twist.

NUTRITIONAL VALUES: Calories: 134, Fat: 6g, Carbs: 17g, Protein: 5g, Sugar: 0g

SPICED ROASTED CHICKPEAS

PREPARATION TIME: 10 min
COOKING TIME: 30 min
MODE OF COOKING: Roasting
SERVINGS: 4

INGREDIENTS:

- 2 cans (15 oz. each) chickpeas, drained

- and rinsed
- 1 Tbsp olive oil
- 1 tsp smoked paprika
- 1/2 tsp ground cumin
- 1/4 tsp chili powder
- 1/4 tsp garlic powder
- Salt to taste

DIRECTIONS:

1. Preheat oven to 400°F (204°C).
2. Pat the chickpeas dry with a clean kitchen towel or paper towels, ensuring they are thoroughly dried.
3. In a bowl, mix the dried chickpeas with olive oil, smoked paprika, cumin, chili powder, garlic powder, and salt, ensuring all chickpeas are evenly coated.
4. Spread chickpeas in a single layer on a baking sheet lined with parchment paper.
5. Roast in the preheated oven for about 30 min, shaking the pan every 10 min to ensure even roasting and crispiness.
6. Remove from oven and let cool slightly before serving.

TIPS:

- For extra crispiness, let the chickpeas cool in the oven with the door slightly open.
- These can be stored in an airtight container for up to a week for a quick snack.
- Experiment with different spices based on your preference, such as turmeric or curry powder for a different flavor profile.

NUTRITIONAL VALUES: Calories: 215, Fat: 8g, Carbs: 29g, Protein: 9g, Sugar: 5g

SPICY AVOCADO AND CHICKPEA TOAST

PREPARATION TIME: 10 min
COOKING TIME: 5 min
MODE OF COOKING: Toasting
SERVINGS: 4

INGREDIENTS:

- 1 ripe avocado, peeled and pitted
- 1 can (15 oz.) chickpeas, rinsed and drained

- 1 small red onion, finely chopped
- 2 Tbsp olive oil
- 1 tsp ground cumin
- 1/2 tsp chili powder
- 1/2 tsp sea salt
- 4 slices of whole-grain bread
- Fresh cilantro leaves for garnish
- Red pepper flakes, to taste

DIRECTIONS:

1. In a medium bowl, mash the avocado using a fork.
2. Add chickpeas to the bowl and coarsely mash them together with the avocado.
3. Stir in chopped red onion, olive oil, cumin, chili powder, and sea salt, blending well.
4. Toast the bread slices until golden and crispy.
5. Spread the avocado and chickpea mixture evenly on each slice of toasted bread.
6. Garnish with fresh cilantro leaves and sprinkle with red pepper flakes if desired.

TIPS:

- For a gluten-free option, use gluten-free bread.
- Add a squeeze of lemon juice to the avocado mixture for an extra zest.
- Customize the spiciness by adjusting the amount of chili powder and red pepper flakes.

NUTRITIONAL VALUES: Calories: 290, Fat: 14g, Carbs: 35g, Protein: 9g, Sugar: 5g

---

SPICY AVOCADO HUMMUS

PREPARATION TIME: 10 min
COOKING TIME: None
MODE OF COOKING: Blending
SERVINGS: 6
INGREDIENTS:

- 2 ripe avocados, peeled and pitted
- 1 can (15 oz.) chickpeas, drained and rinsed
- 2 Tbsp tahini
- 2 cloves garlic, minced
- 1 lemon, juiced
- 1/2 tsp cayenne pepper
- 1/2 tsp ground cumin
- Salt to taste
- 2 Tbsp olive oil
- 1/4 cup fresh cilantro, chopped
- Water, as needed for consistency

DIRECTIONS:

1. In a food processor, combine avocados, chickpeas, tahini, minced

garlic, lemon juice, cayenne pepper, cumin, and salt.

2. Pulse the mixture while slowly adding olive oil until the hummus is smooth and creamy.
3. If the hummus is too thick, slowly add water, a tablespoon at a time, until it reaches your desired consistency.
4. Stir in the chopped cilantro for an added freshness.
5. Transfer the humus to a bowl and serve it chilled or at room temperature.

TIPS:

- Garnish with paprika and a drizzle of olive oil before serving for extra flavor and a colorful presentation.
- Serve with a variety of fresh vegetables or whole-grain crackers for a healthy snack.
- Store in an airtight container in the refrigerator for up to 3 days for best freshness.

NUTRITIONAL VALUES: Calories: 190, Fat: 13g, Carbs: 16g, Protein: 5g, Sugar: 2g

ZESTY AVOCADO AND CHICKPEA HUMMUS

PREPARATION TIME: 10 min
COOKING TIME: 0 min
MODE OF COOKING: Blending
SERVINGS: 4
INGREDIENTS:

- 1 ripe avocado, peeled and pitted
- 1 can (15 oz) chickpeas, rinsed and drained
- 2 Tbsp tahini (sesame seed paste)
- 2 cloves garlic, minced
- Juice of 1 lemon
- 2 Tbsp extra-virgin olive oil
- Salt and pepper to taste
- 1/4 tsp cayenne pepper (optional)
- 1/4 cup fresh cilantro, chopped (for garnish)
- 1/4 tsp paprika (for garnish)

DIRECTIONS:

1. In a food processor, combine the avocado, chickpeas, tahini, garlic, and lemon juice.
2. Process until the mixture becomes smooth and creamy.
3. With the processor running, slowly drizzle in the olive oil until fully incorporated.
4. Season with salt, pepper, and cayenne pepper if using.
5. Transfer the hummus to a serving

bowl and garnish with chopped cilantro and a sprinkle of paprika.

TIPS:

- For a creamier hummus, add a bit more olive oil or a tablespoon of water to adjust the consistency.
- Serve with a variety of raw vegetables such as carrots, celery, and bell peppers for dipping.
- Refrigerate in an airtight container for up to 5 days.

NUTRITIONAL VALUES: Calories: 210, Fat: 14g, Carbs: 17g, Protein: 6g, Sugar: 2g

SPICED ROASTED CHICKPEAS

PREPARATION TIME: 10 min
COOKING TIME: 40 min
MODE OF COOKING: Roasting
SERVINGS: 4
INGREDIENTS:

- 1 can (15 oz.) chickpeas, drained and rinsed
- 1 Tbsp olive oil
- 1 tsp ground cumin
- 1 tsp smoked paprika
- 1/2 tsp chili powder
- 1/4 tsp garlic powder
- Salt and pepper to taste

DIRECTIONS:

1. Preheat your oven to 375°F (190°C).
2. Dry the chickpeas with a clean kitchen towel or paper towels, removing as much moisture as possible.
3. In a bowl, toss the chickpeas with olive oil, cumin, smoked paprika, chili powder, garlic powder, salt, and pepper until evenly coated.
4. Spread the chickpeas on a baking sheet in a single layer.
5. Roast in the oven for 35-40 minutes, stirring halfway through, until crispy and golden brown.

TIPS:

- For extra crispiness, let the chickpeas cool in the oven after turning it off.
- You can store roasted chickpeas in an

airtight container for up to a week, though they are best when fresh.

NUTRITIONAL VALUES: Calories: 134, Fat: 5g, Carbs: 18g, Protein: 6g, Sugar: 3g

6. DINNER

MEDITERRANEAN STUFFED BELL PEPPERS

PREPARATION TIME: 20 min
COOKING TIME: 35 min
MODE OF COOKING: Baking
SERVINGS: 4

INGREDIENTS:

- 4 large bell peppers, tops cut away and seeds removed
- 1 cup quinoa, rinsed
- 2 cups vegetable broth
- 1 Tbsp olive oil
- 1 medium onion, finely chopped
- 3 cloves garlic, minced
- 1 zucchini, diced
- 1 cup cherry tomatoes, halved
- 1/2 cup Kalamata olives, pitted and sliced
- 1/4 cup crumbled feta cheese
- 2 Tbsp pine nuts
- 1 tsp dried oregano
- 1 tsp dried basil
- Salt and pepper to taste
- Fresh parsley, for garnish

PROCEDURE:

1. Preheat oven to 375°F (190°C).
2. Place the cleaned bell peppers in a baking dish.
3. In a medium saucepan, bring the vegetable broth to a boil. Add quinoa, cover, and simmer for 15 min or until all liquid is absorbed.
4. Heat olive oil in a skillet over medium heat. Add onions and garlic, sautéing until onions are translucent.
5. Add zucchini to the skillet and sauté for an additional 5 min.
6. Remove from heat and stir in the cooked quinoa, cherry tomatoes, olives, feta cheese, pine nuts, oregano, basil, salt, and pepper.
7. Spoon the filling into each bell pepper cavity until fully stuffed.
8. Replace the tops of the peppers, or leave them off for a crispy finish.
9. Bake in the preheated oven for 20 min or until the peppers are tender.
10. Garnish with fresh parsley before serving.

TIPS:

- For a vegan version, substitute feta cheese with a vegan cheese alternative or nutritional yeast.
- To enhance the flavors, add a drizzle of balsamic reduction before serving.
- Serve with a side of mixed greens for a balanced meal.

NUTRITIONAL VALUES: Calories: 290, Fat: 10g, Carbs: 42g, Protein: 9g, Sugar: 6g

GINGER-SOY GLAZED SALMON WITH BROCCOLI

PREPARATION TIME: 20 min
COOKING TIME: 15 min
MODE OF COOKING: Grilling
SERVINGS: 4
INGREDIENTS:

- 4 salmon fillets (about 6 oz. each)
- 1 Tbsp olive oil
- 2 Tbsp soy sauce
- 1 Tbsp fresh ginger, minced
- 2 garlic cloves, minced
- 1 Tbsp honey
- 1 tsp sesame oil
- 1 Tbsp rice vinegar
- 2 cups broccoli florets
- Salt and pepper to taste
- Sesame seeds for garnish

DIRECTIONS:

1. In a small bowl, whisk together the soy sauce, ginger, garlic, honey, sesame oil, and rice vinegar to create the marinade.
2. Place salmon fillets in a shallow dish or a resealable plastic bag. Pour half of the marinade over the salmon, coating evenly. Reserve the other half for later use. Marinate for at least 15 minutes in the refrigerator.
3. Preheat the grill to medium-high heat (about 375°F or 190°C).
4. Lightly oil the grill grates. Grill salmon fillets for about 6-7 minutes on each side, or until cooked through and easily flakes with a fork.
5. While the salmon is grilling, heat olive oil in a skillet over medium heat. Add broccoli florets, season with salt and pepper, and sauté until tender-crisp, about 5-7 minutes.
6. Heat the remaining marinade in a small saucepan over medium heat until slightly reduced, about 3-5 minutes.
7. Serve the grilled salmon with sautéed broccoli. Drizzle the reduced marinade over the salmon and sprinkle sesame seeds as garnish.

TIPS:

- Marinate the salmon for longer, up to 1 hour, for more intense flavor.
- Ensure the grill is well-oiled to prevent the salmon from sticking.

- Substitute broccoli with asparagus or green beans for variation.

NUTRITIONAL VALUES: Calories: 295, Fat: 13g, Carbs: 9g, Protein: 34g, Sugar: 5g

LEMON GARLIC ROASTED CHICKEN WITH ASPARAGUS

PREPARATION TIME: 20 min
COOKING TIME: 50 min
MODE OF COOKING: Roasting
SERVINGS: 4
INGREDIENTS:
- 4 chicken breasts (boneless, skinless)
- 1 lb asparagus, trimmed
- 4 Tbsp olive oil
- 4 garlic cloves, minced
- 1 lemon, halved (juice one half, slice the other half)
- 1 tsp salt
- 1/2 tsp black pepper
- 1 tsp dried thyme
- 1 tsp dried rosemary

DIRECTIONS:
1. Preheat the oven to 375°F (190°C).
2. In a small bowl, mix olive oil, minced garlic, lemon juice, salt, pepper, thyme, and rosemary.
3. Place the chicken breasts in a large baking dish and pour half of the lemon garlic mixture over them, ensuring they are well-coated.
4. Arrange the trimmed asparagus around the chicken in the dish. Drizzle the remaining lemon garlic mixture over the asparagus.
5. Place lemon slices on top of the chicken and asparagus.
6. Roast in the preheated oven for about 50 minutes, or until the chicken is fully cooked with an internal temperature of 165°F (74°C) and asparagus is tender-crisp.
7. Remove from oven and let rest for 5 minutes before serving.

TIPS:
- For extra flavor, marinate the chicken breasts in the lemon garlic mixture for 1 hour before cooking.
- Serve with a side of quinoa or brown rice for a complete meal.
- Garnish with fresh parsley for a touch of color and freshness.

NUTRITIONAL VALUES: Calories: 345, Fat: 15g, Carbs: 5g, Protein: 44g, Sugar: 2g

GINGER-LIME BAKED SALMON WITH ASPARAGUS

PREPARATION TIME: 15 min
COOKING TIME: 20 min
MODE OF COOKING: Baking
SERVINGS: 4
INGREDIENTS:

- 4 salmon fillets (6 oz. each)
- 1 Tbsp olive oil
- 2 Tbsp fresh lime juice
- 1 tsp grated ginger
- 2 cloves garlic, minced
- Salt and black pepper to taste
- 1 lb. asparagus, trimmed
- Lime slices, for garnish

DIRECTIONS:

1. Preheat your oven to 400°F (204°C).
2. Arrange the salmon fillets on a baking tray lined with parchment paper.
3. In a small bowl, mix together olive oil, lime juice, grated ginger, minced garlic, salt, and pepper.
4. Brush the mixture evenly over the salmon fillets.
5. Toss the asparagus in the remaining mixture and arrange them around the salmon on the tray.
6. Bake in the preheated oven for 20 minutes, or until salmon flakes easily with a fork and asparagus is tender-crisp.
7. Serve hot, garnished with lime slices.

TIPS:

- Ensure not to overcook the salmon to maintain its moisture and tenderness.
- Garnish with fresh cilantro or parsley for an extra burst of freshness.

NUTRITIONAL VALUES: Calories: 225, Fat: 13g, Carbs: 2g, Protein: 24g, Sugar: 1g

TURMERIC-GINGER GRILLED CHICKEN

PREPARATION TIME: 20 min
COOKING TIME: 15 min
MODE OF COOKING: Grilling
SERVINGS: 4
INGREDIENTS:

- 4 boneless, skinless chicken breasts
- 2 Tbsp olive oil
- 1 Tbsp grated fresh ginger
- 1 Tbsp grated fresh turmeric (or 1 tsp dried turmeric)
- 2 cloves garlic, minced
- Juice of 1 lemon
- 1 tsp salt
- 1/2 tsp black pepper

- Fresh cilantro, chopped, for garnish

DIRECTIONS:

1. In a small bowl, mix together olive oil, ginger, turmeric, garlic, lemon juice, salt, and pepper.
2. Place chicken breasts in a shallow dish or resealable plastic bag.
3. Pour the marinade over the chicken, making sure each piece is evenly coated.
4. Cover and refrigerate for at least 15 minutes, preferably 1 hour, to let the flavors meld.
5. Preheat the grill to medium-high heat (approximately 375°F or 190°C).
6. Grill the chicken for about 7-8 minutes on each side, or until the internal temperature reaches 165°F (74°C).
7. Remove from grill and let rest for a few minutes.
8. Garnish with chopped cilantro before serving.

TIPS:

- If using dried turmeric, ensure it's freshly ground for the best flavor and health benefits.
- Allow the chicken to marinate longer if time permits, up to overnight, to enhance the infusion of flavors.
- Serve with a side of grilled vegetables or a fresh salad for a complete meal.

NUTRITIONAL VALUES: Calories: 210, Fat: 10g, Carbs: 2g, Protein: 26g, Sugar: 0g

LEMON-HERB GRILLED SALMON WITH ASPARAGUS

PREPARATION TIME: 20 min
COOKING TIME: 15 min
MODE OF COOKING: Grilling
SERVINGS: 4
INGREDIENTS:

- 4 salmon fillets (about 6 oz. each)
- 1 bunch of asparagus, trimmed
- 2 lemons, one juiced and one sliced
- 2 Tbsp olive oil
- 4 garlic cloves, minced
- 2 Tbsp fresh dill, chopped
- 2 Tbsp fresh parsley, chopped
- Salt and pepper to taste

DIRECTIONS:

1. Preheat your grill to medium-high heat, approximately 375°F (190°C).
2. In a small bowl, mix olive oil, lemon juice, minced garlic, dill, parsley, salt, and pepper.
3. Brush the salmon fillets and asparagus

with the herb mixture.

4. Place lemon slices on the grill and set the salmon on top of the lemon slices to prevent sticking and add citrus flavor.
5. Grill the salmon for about 6-7 min on each side or until cooked through and easily flakeable with a fork.
6. Concurrently, grill the asparagus alongside the salmon, turning occasionally, until tender and charred, about 7-10 min.
7. Serve the salmon and asparagus garnished with additional fresh herbs.

TIPS:

- Grilling salmon on lemon slices not only adds flavor but also prevents the fish from sticking to the grill grate.
- Keep a close eye on the asparagus to ensure it cooks evenly and doesn't char too much.

NUTRITIONAL VALUES: Calories: 345, Fat: 22g, Carbs: 6g, Protein: 30g, Sugar: 2g

GRILLED POLENTA WITH RATATOUILLE

PREPARATION TIME: 20 min
COOKING TIME: 40 min
MODE OF COOKING: Grilling and simmering
SERVINGS: 4
INGREDIENTS:

- 1 cup polenta
- 4 cups water
- 1 tsp salt
- 1 Tbsp olive oil, plus extra for brushing
- 1 zucchini, diced
- 1 yellow squash, diced
- 1 small eggplant, diced
- 1 red bell pepper, diced
- 1 onion, finely chopped
- 2 cloves garlic, minced
- 1 can (14 oz) diced tomatoes
- 1 tsp dried basil
- 1 tsp dried thyme
- Salt and pepper to taste
- Fresh basil leaves for garnish

DIRECTIONS:

1. Bring water to a boil in a medium saucepan. Gradually whisk in polenta

and tsp salt, reduce the heat to low, and cook, stirring frequently, until thick and creamy, about 20-25 mins.

2. Spread the cooked polenta in a greased baking dish, smoothing the top with a spatula. Allow to cool and set for about 15 mins, then cut into squares.

3. Heat 1 Tbsp olive oil in a large skillet over medium heat. Add onion and garlic, cook until softened, about 5 mins.

4. Stir in the zucchini, squash, eggplant, and red bell pepper. Cook for about 10 mins, until vegetables are just tender.

5. Add the diced tomatoes, dried basil, thyme, and season with salt and pepper. Simmer for another 15 mins until the vegetables are soft and the flavors meld.

6. Preheat the grill to medium-high. Brush polenta squares with olive oil and grill until marked and heated through, about 3-4 mins per side.

7. Serve grilled polenta topped with ratatouille and garnished with fresh basil leaves.

TIPS:

- Ensure the polenta is thoroughly cooled and set before grilling to prevent breaking.
- Add a sprinkle of grated Parmesan over the ratatouille for a cheesy twist.
- Can be served with a side of mixed greens to add freshness.

NUTRITIONAL VALUES: Calories: 290, Fat: 7g, Carbs: 53g, Protein: 7g, Sugar: 10g

ZESTY LEMON HERB CHICKEN WITH ASPARAGUS

PREPARATION TIME: 10 min
COOKING TIME: 30 min
MODE OF COOKING: Baking
SERVINGS: 4
INGREDIENTS:

- 4 boneless, skinless chicken breasts
- 1 lb asparagus, ends trimmed
- 2 lemons, 1 juiced and 1 sliced
- 3 Tbsp olive oil
- 4 cloves garlic, minced
- 1 tsp dried basil
- 1 tsp dried oregano
- Salt and pepper to taste
- Fresh parsley, chopped (for garnish)

DIRECTIONS:

1. Preheat the oven to 400°F (204°C).
2. In a small bowl, mix the olive oil, lemon juice, garlic, basil, oregano, salt,

and pepper.
3. Lay the chicken breasts in a large baking dish.
4. Arrange the asparagus around the chicken in the dish.
5. Pour the olive oil and lemon mixture over the chicken and asparagus, ensuring everything is well coated.
6. Place lemon slices on top of the chicken breasts.
7. Bake in the preheated oven for about 25-30 minutes, or until the chicken is cooked through and the asparagus is tender.
8. Garnish with fresh parsley before serving.

TIPS:
- Ensure the chicken breasts are of even thickness for uniform cooking.
- If desired, add a splash of white wine to the dish before baking for added flavor.
- Serve with a side of quinoa or brown rice to complete the meal.

NUTRITIONAL VALUES: Calories: 275, Fat: 9g, Carbs: 8g, Protein: 36g, Sugar: 3g

7. DESSERT

COCONUT CHIA ALMOND DELIGHT

PREPARATION TIME: 15 min
COOKING TIME: 0 min
MODE OF COOKING: Chilling
SERVINGS: 4
INGREDIENTS:

- 1/4 cup chia seeds
- 1 cup unsweetened almond milk
- 1/2 cup coconut cream
- 2 Tbsp honey (or maple syrup for vegan option)
- 1/2 tsp vanilla extract
- 1/4 cup sliced almonds
- 1/4 cup shredded coconut
- Fresh berries for topping

DIRECTIONS:

1. In a mixing bowl, combine chia seeds, almond milk, coconut cream, honey, and vanilla extract.
2. Whisk thoroughly until the mixture starts to thicken.
3. Cover the bowl and refrigerate for at least 3 hours, or overnight, allowing the chia seeds to gel.
4. Once set, stir the pudding to check consistency. If too thick, stir in additional almond milk to desired consistency.
5. Serve in bowls or glasses, topped with sliced almonds, shredded coconut, and fresh berries.

TIPS:

- For a tropical twist, add a tablespoon of crushed pineapple or mango to the mixture before chilling.
- To make this dessert completely vegan, use maple syrup instead of honey.
- Store in the refrigerator in an airtight container for up to three days.

NUTRITIONAL VALUES: Calories: 215, Fat: 15g, Carbs: 18g, Protein: 4g, Sugar: 10g

AVOCADO LIME CHEESECAKE

PREPARATION TIME: 20 min
COOKING TIME: None
MODE OF COOKING: Freezing
SERVINGS: 8

INGREDIENTS:

- 1 and 1/2 cups raw cashews, soaked for 4 hours and drained
- 2 ripe avocados, peeled and pitted

- 1/2 cup lime juice, freshly squeezed
- 1/2 cup coconut oil, melted
- 1/2 cup maple syrup
- 1 tsp vanilla extract
- Pinch of sea salt
- **For the crust:**
    - 1 cup medjool dates, pitted
    - 1 cup almonds
    - 1/2 tsp sea salt

PROCEDURE:

1. Begin by making the crust. In a food processor, combine the dates, almonds, and sea salt. Pulse until the mixture is finely ground and sticks together when pressed.
2. Press the crust mixture firmly and evenly into the bottom of a lined 8-inch springform pan. Place in the freezer to set while you make the filling.
3. Clean the food processor, then add the soaked cashews, avocados, lime juice, coconut oil, maple syrup, vanilla extract, and a pinch of sea salt. Blend until the mixture is completely smooth and creamy.
4. Pour the filling over the crust and smooth the top with a spatula.
5. Freeze the cheesecake for at least 4 hours, or until firm.
6. Before serving, remove from the freezer and let sit at room temperature for 10-15 minutes to soften slightly.
7. Slice and serve immediately.

TIPS:

- Decorate with thin lime slices or zest before freezing for an extra touch of flair.
- If the cheesecake is too firm after freezing, allow it to thaw slightly before slicing for easier serving.
- For a sweeter crust, you can add an extra tablespoon of maple syrup to the crust mixture.

NUTRITIONAL VALUES: Calories: 350, Fat: 24g, Carbs: 30g, Protein: 6g, Sugar: 18g

NO-BAKE COCONUT CASHEW BARS

PREPARATION TIME: 20 min

COOKING TIME: 0 min (requires 1 hr chilling)

MODE OF COOKING: No-bake

SERVINGS: 12 bars

INGREDIENTS:

- 1 cup raw cashews
- 1 cup desiccated coconut, unsweetened
- 1/2 cup dates, pitted
- 1/4 cup coconut oil, melted
- 1 tsp vanilla extract
- 1/4 tsp sea salt
- Optional: 1/4 cup dark chocolate chips (at least 70% cocoa)

DIRECTIONS:

1. Place the cashews and desiccated coconut in a food processor and pulse until coarsely ground.
2. Add the dates, melted coconut oil, vanilla extract, and sea salt. Process until the mixture sticks together when pressed between your fingers.
3. Press the mixture into an 8x8 inch (20x20 cm) baking dish lined with parchment paper.
4. If using, melt the chocolate chips in a microwave or double boiler and drizzle over the top of the bars.
5. Refrigerate for at least 1 hr or until firm.
6. Cut into 12 bars and serve. Store any leftovers in the refrigerator.

TIPS:

- For a sweeter taste, you can add a tablespoon of honey or maple syrup to the mixture.
- Keep the bars refrigerated as they soften at room temperature due to the coconut oil.
- Sprinkle some crushed nuts on top before chilling for added crunch.

NUTRITIONAL VALUES: Calories: 200, Fat: 15g, Carbs: 15g, Protein: 3g, Sugar: 7g

SPICED AVOCADO CHOCOLATE MOUSSE

PREPARATION TIME: 15 min

COOKING TIME: 0 min

MODE OF COOKING: Blending

SERVINGS: 4

INGREDIENTS:

- 2 ripe avocados, peeled and pitted
- 1/4 cup raw cacao powder
- 1/4 cup pure maple syrup

- 1/2 tsp vanilla extract
- 1/4 tsp cinnamon
- 1/4 tsp cardamom
- A pinch of sea salt
- Fresh berries for garnish (optional)

DIRECTIONS:

1. Place the avocados, cacao powder, maple syrup, vanilla extract, cinnamon, cardamom, and sea salt in a blender.
2. Blend on high until the mixture is completely smooth.
3. Transfer the mousse to serving dishes and refrigerate for at least 30 minutes to set.
4. Garnish with fresh berries before serving, if desired.

TIPS:

- Ensure avocados are ripe for the best flavor and texture.
- For a deeper chocolate taste, add an extra tablespoon of cacao powder.
- Serve chilled for a refreshing dessert option.

NUTRITIONAL VALUES: Calories: 230, Fat: 15g, Carbs: 25g, Protein: 3g, Sugar: 15g

ZESTY ORANGE AND ALMOND FLOUR CAKE

PREPARATION TIME: 20 min
COOKING TIME: 35 min
MODE OF COOKING: Baking
SERVINGS: 8
INGREDIENTS:

- 2 cups almond flour
- 3 large eggs
- 1/2 cup honey
- 1/4 cup coconut oil, melted
- 2 oranges, juiced and zested
- 1 tsp baking powder
- 1/2 tsp salt
- 1/4 cup sliced almonds, for topping

DIRECTIONS:

1. Preheat the oven to 350°F (177°C) and grease a 9-inch round cake pan.
2. In a large bowl, combine almond flour, baking powder, and salt.
3. In another bowl, whisk together eggs, orange juice, orange zest, honey, and melted coconut oil.
4. Gradually mix the wet ingredients into the dry ingredients, stirring until well combined.
5. Pour the batter into the prepared cake pan and sprinkle with sliced almonds.

6. Bake for 35 minutes or until a toothpick inserted into the center comes out clean.
7. Allow to cool in the pan for 10 minutes before transferring to a wire rack to cool completely.

TIPS:
- Ensure all ingredients are at room temperature to help them blend more smoothly.
- Garnish with fresh orange slices for added freshness and a vibrant appearance.

NUTRITIONAL VALUES: Calories: 315, Fat: 23g, Carbs: 23g, Protein: 8g, Sugar: 17g

ALMOND AND COCONUT FLOUR BERRY CRISP

PREPARATION TIME: 15 min
COOKING TIME: 30 min
MODE OF COOKING: Baking
SERVINGS: 6

INGREDIENTS:
- 1 cup mixed berries (blueberries, raspberries, strawberries)
- 1 cup almond flour
- 1/2 cup coconut flour
- 1/4 cup honey
- 1/4 cup coconut oil, melted
- 1 tsp cinnamon
- 1/4 tsp salt
- 1 tsp vanilla extract

DIRECTIONS:
1. Preheat the oven to 375°F (190°C).
2. In a mixing bowl, combine almond flour, coconut flour, cinnamon, and salt.
3. Stir in melted coconut oil, honey, and vanilla extract until the mixture becomes crumbly.
4. Place mixed berries in a greased baking dish.
5. Sprinkle the crumbly flour mixture evenly over the berries.
6. Bake in the preheated oven for about 30 minutes or until the topping is golden and the berries are bubbly.
7. Allow to cool slightly before serving.

TIPS:
- Serve with a dollop of Greek yogurt or coconut cream for added creaminess.
- You can adjust the sweetness by adding more or less honey according to your preference.
- For a nuttier flavor, sprinkle chopped almonds over the topping before baking.

NUTRITIONAL VALUES: Calories: 280, Fat: 18g, Carbs: 24g, Protein: 6g, Sugar: 12g

8. HEALTH SMOOTHIE

GREEN GODDESS DETOX SMOOTHIE

PREPARATION TIME: 10 min

COOKING TIME: 0 min

MODE OF COOKING: Blending

SERVINGS: 2

INGREDIENTS:

- 1 ripe avocado, peeled and pitted
- 1/2 cucumber, peeled and chopped
- 2 cups fresh spinach leaves
- 1 green apple, cored and chopped
- 1 Tbsp chia seeds
- 1 Tbsp freshly squeezed lemon juice
- 1 cup coconut water
- 4-6 ice cubes
- 1 Tbsp honey (optional)

DIRECTIONS:

1. Place all the ingredients, except for honey, in a blender.
2. Blend on high speed until smooth and creamy.
3. Taste and add honey if a sweeter smoothie is desired. Blend again to mix.
4. Pour into glasses and serve immediately.

TIPS:

- Add a scoop of plant-based protein powder to enhance the smoothie for post-workout recovery.
- If the smoothie is too thick, adjust its consistency by adding a bit more coconut water until desired thickness is achieved.
- Freeze the chopped cucumber and green apple before blending for an extra chilled and refreshing smoothie.

NUTRITIONAL VALUES: Calories: 212, Fat: 9g, Carbs: 31g, Protein: 3g, Sugar: 19g

VIBRANT GREENS DETOX SMOOTHIE

PREPARATION TIME: 10 min

COOKING TIME: 0 min

MODE OF COOKING: Blending

SERVINGS: 2

INGREDIENTS:

- 1 cup fresh spinach leaves
- 1/2 cucumber, sliced
- 1 green apple, cored and chopped
- 1 banana, sliced
- 1 Tbsp chia seeds
- 1 Tbsp fresh ginger, grated
- 1/2 lemon, juiced

- 1 cup coconut water

DIRECTIONS:

1. Place all ingredients into a blender.
2. Blend on high speed until smooth and creamy.
3. Pour into glasses and serve immediately.

TIPS:

- For a cooler smoothie, use frozen banana slices.
- If you prefer a sweeter smoothie, add a teaspoon of honey or agave syrup.
- To boost protein content, add a scoop of your favorite plant-based protein powder.

NUTRITIONAL VALUES: Calories: 180, Fat: 2g, Carbs: 40g, Protein: 3g, Sugar: 22g

ANTI-INFLAMMATORY BERRY BLISS SMOOTHIE

PREPARATION TIME: 10 min
COOKING TIME: 0 min
MODE OF COOKING: Blending
SERVINGS: 2

INGREDIENTS:

- 1 cup frozen blueberries
- 1/2 cup frozen raspberries generic placeholder
- 1/2 banana
- 1 Tbsp chia seeds
- 1 Tbsp flaxseed meal
- 1 cup spinach leaves
- 1 cup unsweetened almond milk
- 1 tsp turmeric powder
- 1/2 tsp ginger, freshly grated
- 1 Tbsp honey (optional)

DIRECTIONS:

The step-by-step approach:

1. Place blueberries, raspberries, and banana in the blender.
2. Add chia seeds, flaxseed meal, and spinach leaves.
3. Pour in almond milk to facilitate blending.
4. Sprinkle turmeric and ginger over the other ingredients.
5. Blend on high until the mixture is smooth and creamy.
6. Taste and add honey if a sweeter smoothie is preferred.
7. Blend again briefly to mix the honey through the smoothie.

8. Serve immediately for the best flavor and nutrient retention.

TIPS:

- If the smoothie is too thick, adjust consistency with a bit more almond milk.
- For an extra protein boost, add a scoop of your favorite plant-based protein powder.
- To enhance absorption of turmeric's benefits, include a pinch of black pepper in the blend.

NUTRITIONAL VALUES: Calories: 220, Fat: 4.5g, Carbs: 41g, Protein: 5g, Sugar: 24g

ANTI-INFLAMMATORY BERRY SPICE SMOOTHIE

PREPARATION TIME: 10 min
COOKING TIME: 0 min
MODE OF COOKING: Blending
SERVINGS: 2
INGREDIENTS:

- 1 cup blueberries, fresh or frozen
- 1/2 banana, sliced
- 1 cup spinach leaves, fresh
- 1 Tbsp chia seeds
- 1/4 tsp ground turmeric
- 1/4 tsp ground cinnamon
- 1/2 inch ginger root, peeled
- 1 Tbsp almond butter
- 1 cup unsweetened almond milk
- Ice cubes (optional, if using fresh blueberries)

DIRECTIONS:

1. Place all ingredients, except ice cubes, in a high-powered blender.
2. Blend on high until smooth, about 30 to 45 seconds.
3. If using fresh blueberries, add ice cubes to the blender and pulse until smooth to achieve a chilled smoothie.
4. Pour into glasses and serve immediately.

TIPS:

- If you prefer a sweeter smoothie, add a teaspoon of honey or maple syrup.
- Boost protein by adding a scoop of your favorite plant-based protein powder.
- For extra fatty acids, include a tablespoon of flaxseeds or hemp seeds.

NUTRITIONAL VALUES: Calories: 195, Fat: 8g, Carbs: 29g, Protein: 5g, Sugar: 14g

Green Detox Power Smoothie

PREPARATION TIME: 10 min

COOKING TIME: 0 min

MODE OF COOKING: Blending

SERVINGS: 2

INGREDIENTS:

- 1 ripe avocado, peeled and pitted
- 2 cups fresh spinach leaves
- 1 medium cucumber, peeled and sliced
- 1 green apple, cored and sliced
- Juice of 1 lemon
- 1 tsp grated ginger
- 2 Tbsp chia seeds
- 1 cup coconut water
- Ice cubes (optional)

DIRECTIONS:

1. Combine avocado, spinach, cucumber, apple, lemon juice, and grated ginger in a blender.
2. Add chia seeds and coconut water to the mixture.
3. Blend on high speed until smooth. If the smoothie is too thick, adjust consistency by adding more coconut water or ice cubes until desired texture is achieved.
4. Pour into glasses and serve immediately.

TIPS:

- For an extra protein boost, add a scoop of your favorite plant-based protein powder.
- Enjoy this smoothie in the morning to kickstart digestion and energize your day.
- Keep your ingredients organic where possible to maximize the benefits of detoxification.

NUTRITIONAL VALUES:

- Calories: 210, Fat: 14g, Carbs: 19g, Protein: 4g, Sugar: 7g

28 DAYS MEAL PLAN

WEEK 1	breakfast	snack	lunch	snack	dinner
Monday	Omega Power Smoothie Bowl	Spiced Chickpea Crunch	Healing Ginger-Turmeric Carrot Soup	Zesty Lemon Herb Chicken	Lemon Garlic Roasted Chicken with Asparagus
Tuesday	Anti-Inflammatory Turmeric Oatmeal	Spicy Avocado and Chickpea Toast	Ginger-Spiced Pumpkin Soup	Quinoa & Roasted Vegetable Bowl	Ginger-Lime Baked Salmon with Asparagus
Wednesday	Turmeric Ginger Oatmeal	Zesty Avocado and Chickpea Hummus	Healing Turmeric Ginger Soup	Quinoa Stuffed Bell Peppers	Turmeric-Ginger Grilled Chicken
Thursday	Quinoa & Blueberry Breakfast Porridge	Spicy Avocado Hummus	Gingered Butternut Squash Soup	Lemon Garlic Roasted Chicken with Root Vegetables	Lemon-Herb Grilled Salmon with Asparagus
Friday	Quinoa & Spinach Breakfast Muffins	Spiced Roasted Chickpeas	Healing Ginger Carrot Soup	Quinoa and Roasted Vegetable Bowl	Grilled Polenta with Ratatouille
Saturday	Ginger Pear Oatmeal	Spiced Roasted Chickpeas	Healing Ginger-Pumpkin Soup	Mediterranean Stuffed Bell Peppers	Zesty Lemon Herb Chicken with Asparagus
Sunday	Quinoa & Spinach Power Breakfast	Spicy Avocado and Chickpea Toast	Soothing Ginger Turmeric Soup	Ginger-Soy Glazed Salmon with Broccoli	Quinoa & Black Bean Stuffed Peppers

WEEK 2	breakfast	snack	lunch	snack	dinner
Monday	Spiced Quinoa & Chia Breakfast Bowl	Green Goddess Detox Smoothie	Healing Turmeric Lentil Soup	Quinoa & Roasted Vegetable Bowl	Ginger-Lime Baked Salmon with Asparagus
Tuesday	Coconut Chia Almond Delight	Vibrant Greens Detox Smoothie	Healing Ginger Pumpkin Soup	Quinoa Stuffed Bell Peppers	Turmeric-Ginger Grilled Chicken
Wednesday	Avocado Lime Cheesecake	Anti-Inflammatory Berry Bliss Smoothie	Healing Ginger-Pumpkin Soup	Lemon Garlic Roasted Chicken with Root Vegetables	Lemon-Herb Grilled Salmon with Asparagus
Thursday	No-Bake Coconut Cashew Bars	Anti-Inflammatory Berry Spice Smoothie	Healing Turmeric Lentil Soup	Quinoa and Roasted Vegetable Bowl	Grilled Polenta with Ratatouille
Friday	Spiced Avocado Chocolate Mousse	Green Detox Power Smoothie	Healing Ginger Pumpkin Soup	Mediterranean Stuffed Bell Peppers	Zesty Lemon Herb Chicken with Asparagus
Saturday	Zesty Orange and Almond Flour Cake	Spicy Avocado Hummus	Healing Ginger-Pumpkin Soup	Ginger-Soy Glazed Salmon with Broccoli	Quinoa & Black Bean Stuffed Peppers
Sunday	Almond and Coconut Flour Berry Crisp	Zesty Avocado and Chickpea Hummus	Healing Turmeric Lentil Soup	Lemon Garlic Roasted Chicken with Asparagus	Quinoa & Roasted Vegetable Bowl

WEEK 3	breakfast	snack	lunch	snack	dinner
Monday	Quinoa & Spinach Power Breakfast Bowl	Spiced Chickpea Crunch	Healing Ginger-Turmeric Carrot Soup	Zesty Lemon Herb Chicken	Lemon Garlic Roasted Chicken with Asparagus
Tuesday	Omega Power Smoothie Bowl	Spicy Avocado and Chickpea Toast	Ginger-Spiced Pumpkin Soup	Quinoa & Roasted Vegetable Bowl	Ginger-Lime Baked Salmon with Asparagus
Wednesday	Anti-Inflammatory Turmeric Oatmeal	Zesty Avocado and Chickpea Hummus	Healing Turmeric Ginger Soup	Quinoa Stuffed Bell Peppers	Turmeric-Ginger Grilled Chicken
Thursday	Turmeric Ginger Oatmeal	Spicy Avocado Hummus	Gingered Butternut Squash Soup	Lemon Garlic Roasted Chicken with Root Vegetables	Lemon-Herb Grilled Salmon with Asparagus
Friday	Quinoa & Blueberry Breakfast Porridge	Spiced Roasted Chickpeas	Healing Ginger Carrot Soup	Quinoa and Roasted Vegetable Bowl	Grilled Polenta with Ratatouille
Saturday	Quinoa & Spinach Breakfast Muffins	Spiced Roasted Chickpeas	Healing Ginger-Pumpkin Soup	Mediterranean Stuffed Bell Peppers	Zesty Lemon Herb Chicken with Asparagus
Sunday	Ginger Pear Oatmeal	Spicy Avocado and Chickpea Toast	Soothing Ginger Turmeric Soup	Ginger-Soy Glazed Salmon with Broccoli	Quinoa & Black Bean Stuffed Peppers

WEEK 4	breakfast	snack	lunch	snack	dinner
Monday	Spiced Quinoa & Chia Breakfast Bowl	Green Goddess Detox Smoothie	Healing Turmeric Lentil Soup	Quinoa & Roasted Vegetable Bowl	Ginger-Lime Baked Salmon with Asparagus
Tuesday	Coconut Chia Almond Delight	Vibrant Greens Detox Smoothie	Healing Ginger Pumpkin Soup	Quinoa Stuffed Bell Peppers	Turmeric-Ginger Grilled Chicken
Wednesday	Avocado Lime Cheesecake	Anti-Inflammatory Berry Bliss Smoothie	Healing Ginger-Pumpkin Soup	Lemon Garlic Roasted Chicken with Root Vegetables	Lemon-Herb Grilled Salmon with Asparagus
Thursday	No-Bake Coconut Cashew Bars	Anti-Inflammatory Berry Spice Smoothie	Healing Turmeric Lentil Soup	Quinoa and Roasted Vegetable Bowl	Grilled Polenta with Ratatouille
Friday	Spiced Avocado Chocolate Mousse	Green Detox Power Smoothie	Healing Ginger Pumpkin Soup	Mediterranean Stuffed Bell Peppers	Zesty Lemon Herb Chicken with Asparagus
Saturday	Zesty Orange and Almond Flour Cake	Spicy Avocado Hummus	Healing Ginger-Pumpkin Soup	Ginger-Soy Glazed Salmon with Broccoli	Quinoa & Black Bean Stuffed Peppers
Sunday	Almond and Coconut Flour Berry Crisp	Zesty Avocado and Chickpea Hummus	Healing Turmeric Lentil Soup	Lemon Garlic Roasted Chicken with Asparagus	Quinoa & Roasted Vegetable Bowl

9. BASICS HOLISTIC HEALING MEDICINE

Introduction to Holistic Medicine

As dawn breaks over a lush landscape, the true essence of holistic medicine begins to shine through, revealing a world where every plant, every breath, every moment of meditation contributes to a grand, balanced tableau of health and wellness. This approach, rooted in the most ancient traditions, sees the individual not merely as a collection of symptoms to be treated in isolation but as a complete entity where mind, body, and spirit are intricately connected.

Holistic medicine invites us to view health through a broader lens, one that encompasses the entirety of our being. It is a call to step back from the precipice of reactionary medicine, where the focus is often on battling disease after it arises, to a more proactive stance that nourishes and supports health at the most fundamental levels.

The journey into holistic health does not begin with a diagnosis, nor does it follow a standardized path. It begins with an understanding, an acknowledgment that every individual is unique, with distinctive needs and an inherent ability to heal and maintain balance. This personalized approach stands in quiet defiance of the one-size-fits-all strategy that characterizes much of modern medicine.

The Roots of Holistic Medicine

The story of holistic medicine is as old as humanity itself, woven into the very fabric of human history. It draws on the rich tapestry of all cultures, from the Ayurvedic traditions of India, with its deep understanding of energy and constitution, to the shamanic healing practices of indigenous tribes, which see the human being as an integral part of the larger ecosystem. These ancient practices underscore the belief that healing comes not from outside interventions but from aligning oneself with the natural rhythms of life.

In these traditional societies, healers were often the keepers of holistic wisdom, understanding that a disturbance in one facet of life could ripple across the entire being. They knew that emotional distress could manifest as physical illness, that spiritual disconnection could lead to mental fatigue, and that restoring harmony might require remedies ranging from herbs to heart-to-heart talks under the starlit sky.

Embracing Modern Insights

As the wheel of time has turned, holistic medicine has not stood still. It has absorbed insights from modern science, integrating tools that enhance our understanding of how the human body works and interacts with its environment. From the development of biochemical profiles to advances in understanding how our brains process emotions, modern research has provided valuable tools that enhance the holistic approach, allowing for a more nuanced understanding of health.

However, holistic medicine's true strength lies not just in integrating modern advances but in its capacity to respect and incorporate these without losing sight of its core principles: balance, wellness, and prevention. It serves as a bridge between the ancient and the modern, offering healing strategies that are as relevant today as they were thousands of years ago.

A Tapestry of Techniques

At the heart of holistic medicine lies a diverse array of practices, each tailored to the individual's unique needs. These might include nutritional counseling, where food becomes more than just fuel—it becomes medicine, capable of healing, restoring, and balancing. Or alternative therapies such as acupuncture, which taps into the body's energy pathways to restore health, and chiropractic treatments, that align the body's structure to improve function and promote health.

Mindfulness and meditation are also pillars of holistic health, offering powerful tools for managing stress and enhancing emotional resilience. By fostering a deep, serene connection with the present moment, these practices help individuals find peace in the now, often leading to profound insights about their health and happiness.

Integrating Into Everyday Life

The beauty of holistic medicine lies in its adaptability; it's not confined to the walls of a clinic or the pages of a medical textbook. Instead, it extends into every aspect of day-to-day life. It prompts us to take a closer look at our environment, our habits, our stresses, and our joys. It encourages us to ask questions: How does the food I eat affect my mood? How does my mood affect my physical health? How do my relationships impact my emotional well-being?

In answering these questions, holistic medicine offers more than just health guidance; it offers a philosophy for living. It encourages an active partnership with our bodies, an ongoing dialogue in which care and listening are mutual. It invites us to see health not as a static state but as a dynamic process, a journey that is both personal and universal.

Conclusion: A Call to Harmonious Living

Holism is more than a medical practice; it is a way of life that respects the interconnectedness of all things. It sees the individual as an integral part of the universe, interconnected with the cycles of nature and the flow of life. This comprehensive approach not only promotes a healthier, more fulfilled life but also fosters a deep sense of connection with the broader world, encouraging us to live with awareness, purpose, and joy. By embracing holistic medicine, we embark on a path that is both ancient and new, a journey that respects the wisdom of the past while embracing the possibilities of the future. It is a path of discovery, healing, and ultimately, deep and enduring health.

Natural Remedies and Treatments

In the gentle, nurturing bosom of Mother Nature lies a rich pharmacy, an age-old cache of botanical wonders that have healed generations through the centuries. These natural remedies and treatments are the very heartbeat of holistic healing, drawing not from synthetics but from the Earth itself. As we explore this green pharmacy, we discover that each leaf, root, and flower carries within it the story of a potential cure, a story passed down through time to heal, soothe, and restore.

At the very essence of holistic medicine is the utilization of nature's bounty as a means to heal the body. Ancient civilizations understood the importance of these natural elements, weaving them into their daily lives and health practices with a deep-seated reverence for their power and potential. Today, as we seek to reconnect with these traditional roots, we find not only a rich history but also a validated approach through modern scientific research that echoes what the ancients always knew.

Harnessing Herbal Wisdom

Imagine strolling through a vibrant garden, each plant offering a unique health benefit. Lavender, for instance, isn't just aesthetically pleasing with its soft purple hues; it's also a potent remedy for easing stress and improving sleep. This isn't folkloric charm; scientific studies back up its calming, sedative properties. Similarly, echinacea, often seen dotting gardens with its stark, cone-shaped flowers, is more than just ornamental. It's a powerhouse immune booster, widely recognized for its ability to fight colds and respiratory infections.

These plants and many others offer a direct line to improving health without the harsh side effects often associated with chemical treatments. For those who tread the holistic path, turning to these remedies isn't merely a matter of tradition; it's a choice supported by both historical use and contemporary scientific validation.

Essential Oils: Concentrated Plant Power

As we delve deeper into nature's toolkit, we encounter essential oils, those concentrated extracts that capture the essence of plants. Each droplet of oil is a distillation of the plant's life force, its complex biochemical makeup, and healing potential. Take, for instance, peppermint oil, known for its invigorating scent. A dab of peppermint oil on the temples or a whiff from a diffuser can rejuvenate the senses and ease headaches, tapping into the plant's natural compounds that benefit the human body. The science of aromatherapy, which harnesses the scents of these oils, goes beyond mere pleasure. It taps into the limbic system, the part of the brain that influences emotions and memory, suggesting a profound interconnection between scents and physiological responses. This principle is fundamental in holistic healing, reminding us that health is a symphony, and every note—from what we smell to what we ingest—plays a critical part.

Healing From the Ground Up: Roots and Mushrooms

Not all of nature's healers are found at eye level. Some of the most potent remedies lie beneath the surface. Consider the humble turmeric root, with its vibrant orange hue, which contains curcumin, a compound with powerful anti-inflammatory and antioxidant properties. This root, often ground into a fine spice, is a staple in natural medicine cabinets for its multifaceted health benefits, especially related to inflammation and pain.

Similarly, the world of fungi offers remarkable healing capabilities. Mushrooms like reishi and cordyceps are not just food but are also revered in holistic medicine for their immune-boosting and energy-enhancing properties. These natural remedies speak to a profound philosophy within holistic healing: that solutions to modern ailments may be found in the ancient and the natural world.

Integrating Natural Remedies into Daily Life

The integration of these natural remedies into daily life is both an art and a science. It's about more than just knowing which herb can alleviate a headache or which essential oil can calm anxiety; it's about weaving these solutions into a cohesive lifestyle that prioritizes prevention and embraces the body's capacity for self-healing.

This philosophy encourages a proactive approach to health, where everyday choices—be it a cup of ginger tea to aid digestion or a nightly chamomile soak to encourage sleep—become acts of self-care. These practices don't just fight off illness; they enhance day-to-day living, elevating the individual's quality of life through nature's simplicity and purity.

Towards a Sustainable Practice

Embracing natural remedies is also a step towards sustainability, aligning personal health practices with environmental consciousness. By choosing organic, locally-sourced herbs and supplements, individuals not only support their health but also contribute to a healthier planet. This interconnectedness is central to holistic healing—it reminds us that our health is a mirror reflecting the health of our world. In conclusion, natural remedies and treatments represent a vital component of holistic medicine, offering effective, gentle, and sustainable options for maintaining health and treating illness. Whether it's through the calming scent of lavender, the immune-supportive power of echinacea, or the deep-root healing properties of turmeric, these natural solutions embody the holistic principle that true healing considers the whole person—body, mind, and spirit. As we continue to explore and integrate these treasures, we do more than heal ourselves; we reconnect with a tradition that honors the wisdom of nature and the inherent potential within each of us to lead a healthier, more harmonious life.

MIND-BODY CONNECTION

To explore the profound interconnection between the mind and body in holistic medicine is like unfolding a map that leads to the treasure of complete well-being. In our journey through life, we often overlook how deeply our mental state affects our physical health and vice versa. Holistic healing places significant emphasis on this interconnectedness, revealing how our thoughts, emotions, and mental states can influence biological functions and impact our overall health.

The Symphony of Mind and Body

Imagine your body as an orchestra where every cell, every organ, plays its distinct part, and the mind acts as the conductor, shaping the music through its thoughts and emotions. When the conductor is calm and focused, the music flows harmoniously. But if the conductor becomes erratic or distressed, the music might become chaotic. This comparison illustrates the impact of our mental states on bodily health, emphasizing why holistic medicine views treatment as a complete symphony of human existence rather than isolated interventions.

For centuries, traditional healers have understood this dynamic. In ancient India, the Ayurvedic practitioners spoke of a life force connecting the body and mind through channels of energy. In traditional Chinese medicine, the philosophy of Yin and Yang demonstrates the balance of opposing forces, asserting that the health of the mind directly influences the vitality of the body.

Stress: The Common Disruptor

Consider how stress—a predominantly mental factor—manifests throughout the body. When we experience stress, the body doesn't distinguish between a physical threat and a psychological one. It responds by releasing cortisol and adrenaline, hormones that prepare the body for a 'fight or flight' reaction. While beneficial in short bursts, persistent stress keeps these hormones elevated, wreaks havoc in the body, and may lead to issues like hypertension, digestive disorders, and immune suppression.

Holistic practices such as meditation, yoga, or even simpler forms of deep breathing exercises play a crucial role in mitigating stress. These activities encourage the body to enter a state of relaxation, counteracting the stress response, and fostering recovery. Through regular practice, these techniques can not only manage stress but also enhance cognitive function, improve emotional resilience, and promote a general sense of well-being.

Emotional Health and Chronic Illness

The connections between emotional health and physical diseases are increasingly recognized in the scientific community. Consider depression, a condition primarily viewed as mental but often accompanied by fatigue, pain, and various somatic complaints. Similarly, anxiety can accelerate the heart rate and increase blood pressure, contributing to chronic heart conditions.

Holistic healing addresses these overlaps by integrating therapies that soothe the mind to heal the body. This might involve counseling, art therapy, or music therapy—approaches that help process emotions, leading to improvements in physical symptoms. The aim is to heal the person as a whole, recognizing that emotional wounds can manifest physically and need to be treated integrally.

The Placebo Effect: Harnessing Belief in Healing

One of the most fascinating aspects of the mind-body connection is the placebo effect, where individuals experience a real alteration in physiology or symptoms based on their expectations alone, without any specific therapeutic intervention. This phenomenon powerfully underscores the mind's influence over the body, suggesting that our beliefs and expectations can actually contribute to our healing process.

In holistic medicine, this is not seen as mere trickery but as a useful tool in healing. By fostering a positive outlook and a strong belief in the efficacy of their treatment plan, individuals can potentially enhance their own healing process. This mind-over-matter aspect is integral to holistic practices and is leveraged to cultivate an environment where healing is nurtured through positive mental and emotional states.

Integrative Approaches in Mind-Body Healing

In bridging the chasm between alternative healing and conventional medicine, an integrative approach that respects and utilizes the mind-body connection can enhance the effectiveness of medical treatments. For example, biopsychosocial models of care, which consider psychological and social factors along with the biological, are becoming more prevalent. This holistic approach is particularly significant in treatments for chronic illnesses where stress, lifestyle, and mental health play pronounced roles.

Furthermore, practices such as biofeedback, where patients learn to control bodily processes that are normally involuntary, such as heart rate or muscle tension, illustrate how harnessing the power of the mind can lead to profound changes in physical health. These techniques empower patients, giving them direct involvement in their own healing process and encouraging a deeper understanding of their bodies.

Conclusion: Mind and Body as One

In holistic healing, the mind and body are inseparable. By promoting practices that enhance mental wellness and acknowledging the profound effects that the mind can have on the physical body, holistic medicine offers a comprehensive approach to health that transcends the limitations of traditional Western medicine. It teaches us that by nurturing our mental and emotional health, we are in fact taking some of the most powerful steps possible towards achieving overall well-being. As we become more attuned to the nuances of this connection, we unlock new possibilities for healing and health, not only treating ailments but also preventing them, guiding us towards a more balanced, healthful existence where the mind and body harmonize to create a symphony of health.

INTEGRATING HOLISTIC PRACTICES INTO DAILY LIFE

Embracing holistic practices is akin to cultivating a garden; it requires patience, persistence, and a deep understanding of the environment to thrive. Incorporating holistic habits into daily life is not merely about adopting new routines, but rather about shifting perspectives and recognizing the interconnectedness of our physical, mental, and spiritual health. It's about weaving age-old wisdom into the fabric of contemporary living, creating a lifestyle that sustains and nourishes on multiple levels.

Small Beginnings Lead to Lifelong Habits

The beauty of integrating holistic practices into daily life lies in the ease with which small and manageable habits can transform into profound health benefits. You might start the day with a few minutes of meditation, using this time to center your thoughts and prepare mentally and emotionally for the day ahead. This simple act can significantly reduce stress levels, enhance focus, and improve mood, setting a positive tone for the day.

Similarly, the incorporation of gentle, mindful exercises, such as yoga or Tai Chi, can strengthen the body while calming the mind. These activities, rooted in ancient traditions, are not only physically beneficial but also serve as mental and spiritual practices that heighten our sense of well-being.

Creating a Holistic Environment at Home

Your living space plays a crucial role in your health and well-being, influencing your mood and energy levels. Creating a holistic environment at home is about more than just aesthetics; it involves crafting a space that promotes peace, tranquility, and healing. This might involve reducing clutter, which in turn can help reduce mental clutter, or incorporating elements of nature like plants, which clean the air and enhance your connection to the earth.

Focusing on the quality of air, water, and light in your home can also profoundly impact your health. Using air purifiers, ensuring adequate hydration with clean, filtered water, and maximizing natural light can enhance your living space's healing potential, supporting your holistic health journey.

Nourishing the Body with Whole Foods

One of the foundational principles of holistic medicine is the belief that food is medicine. Integrating holistic practices into daily life extends into the kitchen, where making conscious food choices can deeply affect your health. Emphasizing whole, unprocessed foods rich in essential nutrients supports body functions and promotes healing. Each meal is an opportunity to impact your health positively, from choosing organic produce to incorporating anti-inflammatory herbs and spices into your cooking.

Moreover, the act of preparing and consuming food should be mindful, appreciating the flavors, textures, and smells and acknowledging the nourishment it provides. This mindfulness in eating can transform it from mere sustenance to a healing act beneficial to both body and mind.

Integrating Mindfulness Throughout the Day

Mindfulness can infuse every aspect of daily life, not just during set meditation sessions or yoga classes. By remaining present and centered throughout the day, whether while walking, eating, or even communicating, you engage in a continuous practice of mindfulness that can significantly enhance your quality of life.

For instance, taking short mindfulness breaks throughout the day can help reset your focus and relieve stress. These breaks may involve deep breathing exercises, a brief walk, or a few moments of quiet reflection—simple practices that can help maintain balance and prevent the buildup of stress.

Building a Supportive Community

Holistic living isn't only about individual practices; it also involves the community we build around us. Encouraging family members or friends to participate in holistic practices such as group meditation sessions, shared meals using whole foods, or joint nature walks, not only supports your own practices but also fosters a supportive environment conducive to overall well-being.

Moreover, engaging with a broader community of like-minded individuals can provide additional motivation and insight, contributing to your holistic lifestyle. Participation in workshops, classes, or group discussions focused on holistic health topics can offer new perspectives and deepen your commitment to this path.

Embracing Natural Therapies and Remedies

Integrating holistic practices into your life includes the use of natural therapies and remedies for health conditions. By utilizing herbal teas, essential oils, or other natural products, you embrace a preventative approach to health, treating minor ailments naturally before they develop into more significant issues.

This proactive approach not only reduces dependency on pharmaceutical solutions but also empowers you to take control of your health by understanding and utilizing the resources nature offers. It underscores the holistic belief in the body's inherent healing capabilities when supported naturally and sustainably.

Conclusion: A Holistic Path Forward

Incorporating holistic practices into daily life is a journey that extends beyond the boundaries of any single method. It is about creating a lifestyle that respects and promotes the natural balance and harmony between the mind, body, and spirit. By adopting these practices, you lay the groundwork for a life of health, happiness, and fulfillment, deeply rooted in the wisdom of holistic medicine. As we continue to navigate through modern life's challenges, turning to holistic practices provides a beacon of hope and healing—an invitation to live a life that is not only healthier but also richer and more connected to the world around us. Whether through small daily routines, thoughtful adjustments to our living spaces, or the mindful consumption of food, each step on this path brings us closer to achieving the profound wellness and inner peace that holistic medicine promises.

10. CONCLUSION

As we draw near to the conclusion of our exploration into the basics of holistic healing medicine, it is worth reflecting on the profoundly transformative journey we have embarked upon together. Our navigation through a rich tapestry of natural remedies, historical wisdom, and practical applications has been fueled by a shared desire for profound, sustainable health. Let's visualize this chapter of our story not as an end but as a vibrant launching point for future endeavors in wellness.

Throughout this book, we've uncovered the enduring truths of holistic medicine truths that connect our physical health to our environment, our diets, and our innermost states of mind. Every page, every remedy, carries with it the echo of ancient cultures that have thrived on the profound connection between nature and human health. Integrating these holistic practices into daily life doesn't merely add to our existence; it redefines it.

Imagine your journey: each step guided by an intuitive grasp of your body's needs, responding not with harsh chemicals and temporary fixes, but with gentle, natural solutions. You learned to listen—really listen—to the subtle cues of your body, interpreting its signals with a newfound wisdom. This transition from passive healthcare recipient to active, informed participant in your own well-being is the essence of holistic healing; a testament to the empowering potential of knowledge.

We delved into the symbiotic relationship between mental clarity and physical vitality, understanding that a serene mind often forecasts a healthy body. This is a visceral reminder of the importance of reducing stress and enhancing emotional well-being as cornerstones of overall health. Activities like yoga, meditation, and mindful breathing became not just techniques for relaxation but powerful tools for sustaining health.

Consider how our discussion ventured beyond typical health advice, reaching into the very spirit of healing. The focus was never solely on treating symptoms but on nurturing the whole person—mind, body, and spirit. By choosing to incorporate holistic health practices into your day-to-day life, you are setting the stage for a lifelong symphony of health, each note resonating with the natural rhythms of life.

The transformative power of whole foods has been a recurring theme—highlighting nature's pantry as both preventive and therapeutic. These are not just meals; they are messages to our bodies, signals that help us regulate, heal, and thrive. Embracing whole foods is embracing a commitment to treat your body with respect, providing it with the tools it needs to function at its best. Sustainable health practices, as discussed, are not just beneficial for us individually but for our community and our planet. By choosing local, organic produce, reducing waste, and respecting the natural cycle of foods, we align closer with the planet's rhythm and pace. This harmonious living is reflected in our health—clearer skin, better digestion, more energy—tangible rewards for our respectful approach.

Now, poised at the end of this chapter, consider how these principles can be woven into the fabric of your life. Envision applying this knowledge with confidence, shaping your health destiny with each informed choice. The path to wellbeing is uniquely yours, but it is paved with universal truths you've gathered along this journey.

Your toolbox is well-equipped with strategies to harness your body's natural healing potential, reduce your reliance on medications, and address the root causes of illness. You've gained more than information; you've rekindled a relationship with your body and its inherent wisdom.

Reflect on the steps you will take beyond this page. How will you integrate these practices daily? Will you rise with the sun for a morning of yoga, or perhaps end your day with a relaxing herbal tea, reflecting on the gratitude for health? The choices are as abundant as they are joyful.

This journey does not end with the closing of this book. It evolves, grows, and flourishes with each choice you make. Share this knowledge, as health and wellness are not just personal triumphs but communal ones. Encourage those around you, lead by example, and build a community where holistic health is not just an ideal but a customary way of life.

As you continue to walk this path of holistic health, remember that each step is a seed planted not only for your well-being but for the nurturing of generations to come. May your journey be as enlightening as it is enlivening, as you carry forward the torch of holistic healing, illuminating the way for others just as you have found your light. With every breath, every meal, every restful night—you are rebuilding, renewing, and reinvigorating your life. Here's to your health, in its most holistic, vibrant form.

MEASUREMENT CONVERSION TABLE

Volume Conversions

Volume (Liquid)	US Customary Units	Metric Units
1 teaspoon	1 tsp	5 milliliters (ml)
1 tablespoon	1 tbsp	15 milliliters
1 fluid ounce	1 fl oz	30 milliliters
1 cup	1 cup	240 milliliters
1 pint	1 pt	473 milliliters
1 quart	1 qt	946 milliliters
1 gallon	1 gal	3.785 liters

Weight Conversions

Weight	US Customary Units	Metric Units
1 ounce	1 oz	28 grams (g)
1 pound	1 lb	454 grams
1 kilogram	2.2 lbs	1000 grams (1 kg)

Length Conversions

Length	US Customary Units	Metric Units
1 inch	1 in	2.54 centimeters (cm)
1 foot	1 ft	30.48 centimeters

Metric Volume Conversions

Volume	Metric Units	US Customary Units
1 milliliter (ml)	1 ml	0.034 fluid ounce (fl oz)
100 milliliters	100 ml	3.4 fluid ounces
1 liter (L)	1 L	34 fluid ounces
		4.2 cups
		2.1 pints
		1.06 quarts
		0.26 gallon

Metric Weight Conversions

Weight	Metric Units	US Customary Units
1 gram (g)	1 g	0.035 ounces (oz)
100 grams	100 g	3.5 ounces
500 grams	500 g	1.1 pounds (lb)
1 kilogram (kg)	1 kg	2.2 pounds

Temperature Conversions

Temperature	Celsius (°C)	Fahrenheit (°F)
Freezing Point	0°C	32°F
Refrigerator	4°C	39°F
Room Temperature	20°C - 22°C	68°F - 72°F
Boiling Water	100°C	212°F

THANK YOU FOR YOUR PURCHASE

Dear Reader,

Thank you for purchasing my book. I genuinely hope it provides you with value and enjoyment. Your support means the world to me and helps more than words can express.

If you could spare a few moments to leave a review, I would greatly appreciate it. Your honest opinion not only aids me in enhancing my work but also guides future readers in their choices.

As a way of saying thanks, I invite you to scan the QR code below to access exclusive bonus content designed especially for you.

Thank you once again for your encouragement and support.

Warm regards,

Kristine Ariyah

Made in United States
Troutdale, OR
03/11/2025